Becoming
Myself

Becoming
Myself

REFLECTIONS ON

GROWING UP FEMALE

EDITED BY Willa Shalit

New York

Excerpts from "Conscientious Objector" by Edna St. Vincent Millay.
From *Collected Poems*, HarperCollins. Copyright © 1934, 1962 by Edna
St. Vincent Millay and Norma Millay Ellis. All rights reserved.
Reprinted by permission of Elizabeth Barnett, literary executor.

Library of Congress Cataloging-in-Publication Data
Becoming myself : reflections on growing up female / edited by Willa
Shalit.—1st ed.
    p. cm
    ISBN 1-4013-0139-8
    1. Women—Biography.   2. Women in public life—Biography.   3.
Celebrities—Biography.   4. Women authors—Biography.   I. Shalit,
Willa.
HQ1123.B43 2006
920.720973—dc22   2005045639

Hyperion books are available for special promotions and premiums.
For details contact Michael Rentas, Assistant Director, Inventory Operations,
Hyperion, 77 West 66th Street, 12th floor, New York, New York 10023,
or call 212-456-0133.

FIRST EDITION

3   5   7   9   10   8   6   4   2

For my beloved Sky—
it is wondrous to watch you become yourself

And Michael,
my rock

Who would ever think that so much went on in the soul of a young girl?

—Anne Frank

Contents

Contents

Introduction

The women in this collection were asked, simply, to recall a significant memory of growing up female.

They responded generously, with intimate stories of their lives. Instead of the superficial prepackaged blurbs of TV sound bites and press releases, they told stories from their hearts; they told secrets never spoken before. In written essays and interviews they revealed themselves through stories of personal confusion and discovery, pain and overcoming, rejection and celebration.

Each of these women describes her process of self-discovery, leading to a place of confidence and comfort with herself. These honest women speak of independence, nostalgia, violence, beauty, self-knowledge, faith, sex, marriage, and divorce, all viewed through the lens of girlhood and womanhood, told as if to a best friend.

As I read each story, I found that it resonated deeply, one making me laugh and hold life more lightly, another making me weep and feel more deeply; but without exception, each made me feel strengthened and less alone.

This response is the opposite of that which often arises in us when the media presents images of celebrities: We may feel less beautiful, less accomplished. We want to be them, not ourselves. This is a phenomenon with which I'm all too familiar.

As the daughter of writer and *Today* show critic Gene Shalit, who has been broadcast into millions of people's homes for thirty-five years, I grew up in a world of media and celebrity. From an early age, I learned to differentiate between the "on camera" and "off camera" personality.

My father always looks past the media hype to a person's talents, artistry, and human qualities. In an industry built on image, he taught me to value substance, honesty, ethical behavior, and true talent.

I saw that people viewed celebrities from a place of envy and inferiority. Instead of being personally inspired by the great artistry of someone like Sophia Loren, they saw her as an Olympian Goddess, a position they could never attain.

When I was a teenager, I once watched Sophia remove her makeup. As she cleaned her face she was transformed from a distant, beautiful movie star to a physically present, strong woman. Speaking of what she looked like when her face was not painted, she said, "I see the sincerity, the happiness . . . but I must tell you my happiness is not a 'ha-ha' kind of thing: It is an earthy thing. That positive earthiness is my sense of self."

At that moment she sensed that I felt the same earthiness in myself. Rather than making me feel like a little Jewish girl with fat thighs standing next to one of the greatest beauties on earth, the experience brought us closer and gave me strength.

This is a book filled with people without their makeup on, showing their most naked face. Kitty Carlisle Hart, born in 1910, tells of surviving her dominating, and sometimes cruel, mother: "No matter what she did while I was growing up, she couldn't crush me. And I'll tell you why. There was a tiny little core deep inside me, like a little stone, and she couldn't squash it. She couldn't crush it. . . . I sailed through life with a great many handicaps, and now look at me. I'm ninety-three years old, happy as a clam." Her words remind us never to forget our core.

Kate Winslet tells of feeling powerless to stop the media from distorting her image and wanting to shout, "This is the real me!" And I recall my earliest memories of being misunderstood and how furious that made me.

Zane describes avoiding the trap of allowing oneself to be defined by a man. I've been dancing around that trap for years, having a famous father. But, like many of the women in this book, I was lucky enough to have a father who always believed in me and encouraged my independence—in my case, from the day I was born, when he named me for the writer Willa Cather, one of the greatest mavericks in American history.

We all seek connection and inspiration, and the women in this book provide both these things, time and time again. We all need role models, and here they are. Each of us is looking for ways to discover ourselves, or better, to *become* ourselves. The women in these pages offer a myriad of road maps to becoming.

As you read about their girlhoods, their mothers and grandmothers, adventures and lessons learned, I hope you will recall your own, and tell someone your stories of growing up female. Keep the chain of inspiration alive.

IN BECOMING MYSELF, I've discovered that my greatest joy lies in giving. I didn't become myself for myself alone, but rather so that I could support others in living fulfilled lives. Forty percent of the royalties from this book will be given to four worthy organizations: Equality Now, The Family Violence Prevention Fund, Intersect-Worldwide, and V-Day. These groups work tirelessly to give women and girls the means to grow and flourish freely.

Becoming
Myself

Maya Angelou

Born April 4, 1928, in St. Louis, Missouri, Maya Angelou was raised in segregated rural Arkansas. She is a poet, historian, author, actress, playwright, civil-rights activist, producer, and director. She lectures throughout the United States and abroad and has been Reynolds Professor of American Studies at Wake Forest University in North Carolina since 1981. She has published ten bestselling books and numerous magazine articles, which have earned her Pulitzer Prize and National Book Award nominations.

BECOMING A WOMAN IS EXCITING, but it's hard. It's onerous, but it's honorable. It's satisfying, because people know a woman. When a woman is in the room, she doesn't have to talk loudly. She doesn't have to carry a six-gun. But people feel safe around her, all sorts of people, people she doesn't even look like. People whose color may be different and who may call God by different names. People from all generations feel comfortable around a woman. To grow up female with the determination to become a woman is to earn all the plaudits, all the accolades, all the respect that this society has to give. I believe you can't do it alone. I believe you have to have the ideals of women who went before you.

For me, these women are my grandmother, my mother, Pearl S. Buck, Madam Sun Yat-sen, and Edna St. Vincent Millay, a little, wan, white, female poet in the 1920s and '30s who became a recluse.

She wrote a poem that says,

> I shall die, but
> that is all that I shall do for Death.
> I hear him leading his horse out of the stall;
> I hear the clatter on the barn-floor.
> He is in haste; he has business in Cuba,
> business in the Balkans, many calls to make this
>   morning.
> But I will not hold the bridle
> while he cinches the girth.
> And he may mount by himself:
> I will not give him a leg up.
>
> Though he flick my shoulders with his whip,
> I will not tell him which way the fox ran.
> With his hoof on my breast, I will not tell him
>   where
> the black boy hides in the swamp.
> I shall die, but that is all that I shall do for Death;
> I am not on his pay-roll.
>
> I will not tell him the whereabout of my friends
> nor of my enemies either.
> Though he promise me much,

I will not map him the route to any man's door.
Am I a spy in the land of the living,
that I should deliver men to Death?
Brother, the password and the plans of our city
are safe with me; never through me Shall you be
overcome.

I've drawn from women in every culture and folk tale that I've read about. The great philosophers—European and Asian and American and African—have taken the wisdom from their grandmothers, mothers, fathers, and grandfathers that was spoken in common "kitchen" or "plantation" talk. They put the content into formal language, and those become philosophical statements of great pith and moment. The truth is the farmer, the peasant, the slave, the workman, and the workingwoman knew that birds of a feather flock together long before Shakespeare said, "Those friends thou hast, and their adoption tried, / Grapple them to thy soul with hoops of steel." They said, "Don't look down and bring somebody up. Look up and pull yourself up." My grandmother used to say, "It's almost impossible to make the richest clothes fit a miserable man." Listen to them without the trappings of academic ignorance. What they have to say is not all that important. It doesn't sound like it's Havelock Ellis, Kant, or Hegel? It doesn't sound as if it's Freud or Rollo May? Well, that's really stupid. If you sit there long enough, you'll hear "mother wit" that is applicable.

I believe that very few people grow up. Most people grow older, but growing up is challenging. Many people get older, honor their credit cards, matriculate into and graduate out of schools, get married and have children. They call that growing up, maturing. It's not. It is simply growing old. One has to assume responsibility for the time one takes up and the space one occupies. To grow up is to stop putting blame on parents. To grow up is to care not only about one's own self but about somebody else's, somebody yet to come. To grow up is to be in a constant state of forgiving. Forgiving yourself for not knowing better, or for knowing better and not doing better, and then releasing people from your own anger and angst. You must stop carrying them around in their ignorance and stupidity and cruelty, giving them purchase on your back, and always having them to poke and to pinch and to carry blame.

Growing up female is difficult. I have a son, and I was with him almost every day of his growing up, but I don't know what that was like, any more than he could know or anybody could know what it cost me to have a monthly period and not be able to explain why. I believe it's equally difficult for a male to grow up, but he may have more help because more men are empowered than women. When he's about fifteen or sixteen and doesn't know what to do with his hands because they're so big, his father and the president of the company and the principal of the high school and the president of the university and the chancellor have been there. They have sympathy for him and can help him. Many times the only people women can identify with are not people in power.

I would encourage a girl who is at that place in life to see herself as she would like to be. To try to envision herself with power. I married a man once because he was a builder. Part of why I married him stemmed from the fact that he was so intelligent. I said I would like to build, but I could never. He said building has nothing to do with physical strength and certainly nothing to do with gender. Building has to do with your insight and determination. He said that if you can see it, you can build it. See it in your mind's eye, see every part of it from the foundation up; then you can build it. That's true for a young woman. See yourself. No matter what the world is saying around you, imagine yourself with power. Try to see yourself with power. Not power so that you can get even with anybody else. Power so that you can become even with your vision.

Joy!
Maya Angelou

Janis Ian

Janis began her musical career at an early age, playing both piano and guitar. When she was fifteen years old, her song of teenage interracial love, "Society's Child," thrust her onto the national stage. Her debut album, released in 1967, brought her the first of nine Grammy nominations. Her single "At Seventeen" sold more than a million copies. After a performing hiatus from 1982 to 1992, she returned to writing and touring. In 2003, she co-edited Stars: Stories Based on the Lyrics of Janis Ian. *Also that year, she married her partner of fourteen years, criminal defense attorney Patricia Snyder.*

I HAD A VERY SUPPORTIVE FAMILY who really believed that intellectual curiosity was to be encouraged, if not demanded, so I was into everything—books, baseball, bicycles, pianos, guitars, puppets, you name it.

When I was eight or nine, my family didn't have much money, so whatever I wanted beyond the bare necessities for school, I had to buy myself. Since I always wanted paper and pens and books, there was a constant struggle to make some money. I baby-sat from the time I was old enough to, and I cleaned people's garages and yards.

Then I realized I could have a paper route once I got a bike, but when I applied, they told me that they didn't give them to girls. So I talked to a couple of the boys. One of them had a brother who had a paper route, and he wanted to make more money. I said, "Well, how about if you give me your paper route, and then I'll give you back some of the money?" It worked out really well for everybody.

In my family, Dad cooked as well as cleaned, and Mom took out the garbage as well as drove the car. Everybody did whatever was necessary, which is very much the way my dad was raised. He grew up on a farm, and on a farm you have to know how to do everything. There was never that male-female division of labor that you see in some families. My brother and I both did the same chores, we both had the same things. I wanted blocks and fire trucks, and I got those.

My mother's family were European Jews who came to America. Very traditional. Her mother stayed home, and her father went out to work and gave his wife all the money at the end of every week. But Mom really was one of the very early women's liberationists, because both she and my dad had no use for any of that nonsense about girls not being as capable as boys in certain areas. I don't know where she got her liberal attitude toward child raising, except that she's a very, very smart lady. She read Dr. Spock from cover to cover a hundred times.

Men just don't think like women. I think they're hard-wired differently. I'm convinced it's genetic, because the most sensitive, wonderful middle-aged guy I know, my uncle, is like that, and my brother is certainly like that. They think differently. They're totally incomprehensible. There's nothing wrong with that. I think it's fine if we can all say we're all really different but we deserve the same rights.

When my ex-husband told me that he didn't make beds, I said, "Well, unless you want to sleep on the floor, that's what you'll be doing here." I don't have any patience with that mind-set, because to me it wastes a lot of valuable time and energy. I remember my uncle, who worked with what they used to call alternative lifestyles, talking to me in the early 1970s about a song I did called "You Got Me on a String." It's very much a period piece and talks about, "If my man beats me, robs me blind, as long as he doesn't leave me, I don't mind." My uncle came backstage and said to me, "You know, you really shouldn't be singing that. These girls are looking up to you, and that's just sending a really bad message." And that was early—1972 or 1973.

I noticed a lot of it as a performer. Boys didn't have to wear makeup, which means that they had half as big a suitcase as I had to tote around; it was assumed that I would wear makeup. When I didn't, people thought I was sick—physically ill. Stage lighting is not geared toward makeup-free faces, but it doesn't matter if you're a boy. As for clothing, I remember doing the *Tonight* show, and I had to wear a dress. I thought, *Well, this sucks.* I think, personally, that I look really stupid playing guitar in a dress. I was sixteen back then.

Times have really changed. The assumption was in those days that if you didn't want to grow up and get married and have a family, you were really weird. At least if you were a woman. I remember there were bachelors in my family and among their friends, and nobody thought anything of it. But if a woman was unmarried and in her thirties or forties, it was considered very strange, very negative. I remember a great quote from back then. Somebody said, "Why is it so many gay women have such a hard set to their chins?" And the answer was, "Because they know that no man will bail them out."

I first fell in love when I was twenty. There's an astonishment, I think, at any age when you're in love, that horrible, heady, desperate feeling that you can't get enough of the person, but it's always too much. There's all the hope when you're young of the promise of love being forever, that the person is the one who really understands you, who knows everything about you. I think it takes a certain level of maturity to come to the point where you understand that even if they don't always understand you, that even though they don't always know you, you can still love somebody very much. When you're young, you're really looking for perfection, and perfection at that age is usually a mirror of yourself.

It's a very complicated thing, being gay and being in love, or it was back then, anyway. The woman I was in love with, her family was never told point-blank. My family knew, and they were fine, but her family would not have been. Then I was outed in the *Village Voice* in 1976 when we were still living together. I'm sure that that caused some consternation. There was a writer whose purpose in life at that time, this gay guy, was to out as many people as possible.

I don't remember his name. He went on a rampage for a few months, and he outed me and Elton and Bowie and a whole mess of people. It freaked me out for a couple of days, partly because I just didn't want to be dealing with it. I was young, and I really didn't want to be dealing with the inevitable questions that would arise. Even when I came out myself in 1992, 1993, and there was all this press, I tried to be very clear in my shows that this was not about excluding anyone. It's always been a worry for me that something like that will get everybody so off topic that they'll forget about what it is I do.

I went through a period when I was about thirty-eight, thirty-nine, or forty when I realized that I was never going to have a hit record again and nobody was going to invest that kind of money in me again. I found myself on the verge of becoming really bitter about it. It was hard walking through that, trying to make the transition to, "OK, if I'm never going to have a hit record again, since that's been the driving goal of my life for decades, what am I going to be when I grow up?" Hopefully, when you realize things like that, you use the realization to move yourself forward instead of backward. I think that's a really important thing, but I don't think you can do it until you again hit a certain level of maturity. I used to resent it so much when adults would tell me, "You won't understand until you're older," but there are an awful lot of things I now realize that they were absolutely right about—and that I could not possibly have understood until I grew up.

I think the big difference between then and now is that

we now all have a vocabulary for things attached to growing up as a female. When I was eight or nine years old, there was no phrase "women's liberation." There was no "equal pay for equal work." Those weren't in the popular lexicon, they weren't subjects you thought about; you just assumed that what you saw on TV in Beaver's house was the way everybody's life was. I knew it wasn't, because my family's life wasn't like that, but I'd say that pretty much everyone else I knew thought that way. So I think at first you can't discuss something until you have a language for it. You can't really think about something until you give it a name. First there's the language, and then, from my own personal viewpoint, there's maturity. There's the concept that there are things that I know now because of my age that give me the right, because of my age and experience, to speak out within the framework of that language in ways that probably wouldn't have occurred when I was younger.

The one thing I would say to girls is, don't settle. This country was founded by women like my grandmothers, who never settled for the life that they had before they threw it away to come here. To me, it's criminal to insist that a girl settle because she's a girl. So if somebody tries to do that to you, put them in jail.

Suzanne Malveaux

Suzanne Malveaux is a CNN White House correspondent and one of the rotating panelists on that network's weekly current-events program On the Story. *Before moving to CNN, she worked as a general-assignment correspondent for NBC News. Prior to that, she did general-assignment reporting for WRC-TV in Washington, D.C., and from 1991 to 1994 worked in the same capacity for FXT-TV and New England Cable News in Boston. She graduated from Harvard University with a bachelor's degree in sociology and has a master's degree in broadcasting from Columbia University. She is an active competitor in triathlon events.*

IT IS A STRANGE EXPERIENCE to be so close to someone that you cannot distinguish where your life begins and the other's ends. That's the way it was growing up with my twin sister, Suzette.

In early childhood, I remember the foot giving way, the slip, and then the tumble down the moving stairs, but I can't tell you whether I was the one who fell down the escalator or whether I was watching my sister take the spill in front of me. All I know is that to this day we both hesitate before we get on an escalator.

My sister and I are both very much alike and very different, as most twins are. But what has shaped my life, in the most profound way, is our bond as sisters. From the moment we were born, we shared our own language. My mother recalls a time when we were infants and spoke only to each other, oblivious to those around us.

Our teachers thought there must have been something in the water or some tyranny in our parents that made us so driven. We were crazy kids. Blowing on clarinets for hours, breaking boards in karate classes, doing all the extra-credit projects we could, earning an A+ grade of 110 percent.

We were the shortest and smallest in our class. And while we indulged in typical girl activities, we delighted in proving that we could take on the boys. We took out the trash, worked the barbecue—we even joined the Boy Scouts!

I don't know what possessed us as little girls to challenge the status quo. My mother had no idea where it came from. But what I do know is that my relationship with my sister is what gave me the confidence to be myself. We thought we could do anything.

Twenty years later, I found myself challenging that notion in the cold waters of Wisconsin's Lake Pewaukee in my first triathlon. When that whistle blew, hundreds of us with matching swim caps and wetsuits plunged into the water. All of my focus was on getting to the shore on the other side. But soon thick seaweed began wrapping around my legs, pulling me down. I started to swallow water, sink, and panic. Once I struggled free, the challenge of following the swimmers out front comforted me. As I neared the shore, however, I was startled by a man with a bullhorn in a rescue boat calling out to me to ask if I was OK. I did not understand his concern until I looked back and realized there was no one behind me. I was dead last! When I hit the shore and jumped on my bike, I was determined to catch up, but much of the rest of the race I spent alone. By the time I started the run portion, the organizers were picking up the traffic cones, and many participants who had finished were drinking beers and packing up their cars to go home. But when I approached the finish line, the crowd began to cheer, and I could feel that the victory was in the trying, not the winning. I would have never imagined being so happy to come in in last place. My sister has always been there with her "Go, Goddess" sign cheering me on during my crazy athletic events.

What gives me the courage to speak to millions today is that my first language was one I spoke only with my sister.

Brooke Shields

Born and raised in New York City, Brooke Shields began her career as a child model. Her first major film role was in the 1977 Louis Malle film Pretty Baby, *in which her character lives in a brothel with her mother. She graduated from Princeton University with a degree in French literature. She has appeared on Broadway a number of times, making her debut as Rizzo, the leader of the Pink Ladies in* Grease. *Between the years of 1980 and 1985, she appeared on more than four hundred magazine covers, including being featured once on the cover of* Time *and on the cover of* Life *on three different occasions. She is the author of the memoir* Down Came the Rain: My Journey Through Postpartum Depression *and has served as an ambassador for the Ronald McDonald House.*

WHEN I WAS A YOUNG GIRL, movies were everything to me. We went religiously. My mom would drive me to the movie theater, and I would sit in the front seat of the car, but on the way home I would sit in the back. I would lean my head against the window and go through the whole story again and what character I was in that movie. And I would take it from the ending and go further and do the story in my head. It became my own relationship with movies, which to me were the ultimate escape.

I don't think I ever really was a "child" child. I was made into a sort of icon of sexuality, simultaneously thought of as the virgin, *which I was,* yet always on the cover of *Vogue* looking much older and sexual. The object of affection and fantasy. I look back and remember my defiance—not letting the system get the better of me and playing whatever role I needed to play to survive on my terms.

Everything was a role. You do it and then you take it all off, you put your jeans on and you go back home and you return to that role. My role was a "good girl"—take care of Mom, do it right, have everybody like you. I think that eventually I became a mockery of it. I learned the ways of seduction, which are much more permissible as a female. All I had to do was one little thing and the audience would roar. I thought, *Isn't that interesting? This can really be abused.* It's power, a great deal of power. I don't think I was mature enough to use it as a weapon. It did scare me just a little bit. Being a female was what gave me a lot of power. Growing up with a single mom, two females all the time, there was a lot of power in that house.

Being the child of an alcoholic, I was very much a parent. Even when I was very young, my first concern was my mom's welfare—how she would take something, what her feelings would be. The good that my mom taught me was really good. She taught me to have integrity. Whether she was capable of practicing what she preached, I'm not sure. But I did see it in her, and I was able to sweep the other horrible side of her under the carpet.

When I got pregnant the first time, I lost the baby. I had to stay around the house for a long time, so I decided to go through box after box after box of press clippings. What the press said about me and my mother was so negative and so horrible, what they said about how little talent I had, it was so hurtful that I got really insecure and sad. Then I started thinking they were right. What a horrible life I had, and how horrible my mother was. But the truth of the matter is, no one will ever really understand what it was like to be me. Hollywood is an industry that predicates itself on negating what someone actually is, and I would never want to subject my daughter to it.

When my mother first saw my baby daughter, Rowan, I think she was really thrown for a loop. There's a picture of her covering her mouth—she was in such shock. I don't think my mother ever saw me as separate from her. Because I came from her, she saw me as an extension of herself. I didn't want to do the same thing with my child. My mom's way of mothering is nothing like the way I instinctually feel, the way I want to mother. I've been unable to differentiate myself from my mother for so many years, for so many reasons, that I thought having my own child would bring us closer. But what it's actually done is to define me as a separate entity. I wanted to find out what sex the baby was and I wanted to pick a name before she was born, because I knew I needed to identify with her as an independent individual. I spent so much time in my head thinking, *She's her own person—she's an individual.*

I didn't have a bond with Rowan for months. I had no connection with her. I thought the baby knew more than I did, that she couldn't possibly need me. That she would just probably reconnect with me when she had it all figured out. Rowan terrified me, because I wasn't sure I liked her. I would think, *I'm supposed to love you? You're born, and I'm just supposed to love you?*

I believe you always want your mother when you have a baby. When you see your parent for the first time as not having all the answers, and yet not knowing what the answers are yourself, it's disorienting. After I had Rowan, my mother was visibly unable to help me, to comfort me. I used to think my mother could make the rain. And she could. So here she was, not doing it, and I was sitting there just shocked. I sort of flattened. I was just level. And then I found my way, and Rowan found her way. She was beginning to respond to me. I started calling her by her name instead of "the baby." I continued breast-feeding through thrush, through her rejecting me, through her pushing me away, through my getting sick. I forced myself to continue, because I needed to bond with her.

I was adamant about being consistent with Rowan. I've never known a life that wasn't bohemian: You eat dinner at ten o'clock, you sleep all day, you wake up at night, you do whatever. I never really liked it, but it's familiar to me. With my daughter, I really want her to know that she can count on bath time and bedtime, and she works better with it.

Rowan was sick recently, and I asked my mom for help. I didn't really want her in my work environment again, because I didn't want to feel like a kid. When I'm around my mom, I kind of regress. But Rowan needed comfort, and I couldn't hold her all the time. Mom had to watch me, to see what I do to comfort Rowan. And I said, "Mom, just hold her tight and hum, and she'll settle in." She stayed in my mom's arms. It was so healing for me to see.

Brooke Shields

Lynn Goldsmith

Lynn Goldsmith is an award-winning photographer whose work has appeared in Life, Newsweek, Time, Rolling Stone, Sports Illustrated, People, Elle, Interview, US, Paris Match, *and a number of books. Her subjects include entertainment personalities, sports stars, film directors, authors, flowers, and nature. In the early 1980s, Lynn detoured from the worlds of both photography and film to become a recording artist. She has written songs with artists such as Sting, Steve Winwood, Todd Rundgren, and Nile Rodgers.*

MY EXPERIENCE OF THE WORLD as a child did not come from having a traditional family. It was spent basically in the company of women: my sister, my mother, my aunt, and her daughter. Both my cousin and I had fathers who were gone by the time we were four. Her father had passed away, and my parents were divorced. My older sister was the boss. My mother behaved like the character *Auntie Mame* in the 1958 film. She would tell us, "Live! Live! Live!" I always thought that was the female spirit. She worked, enjoyed life, and instilled in me the idea that one didn't have to think we were put on this earth to find a man, get married, and live happily or unhappily ever after. I never had any inkling that there was this feminine aspect whose path in life was to follow the rules and obey. That was not in my vocabulary.

I remember very clearly thinking I was luckier than the other kids in my school or the kids on my block. When I saw the movie *Little Women*, it stuck in my mind. I felt that my home, because it was all women, didn't have the kind of energy that seemed to be in the conventional households I visited, particularly the house of my best friend, Lynn Wilson. We were the same age and we spelled our names the same way. She had three brothers. I didn't like all their arguing. I felt that much of the male energy in her house was about squashing her. If we were playing at something, her brothers would put her down. I didn't have that kind of oppressiveness, which I associated with having a father or brothers. I thought it was far more perfect to live in a world of women.

I was always observing people. I wanted to take things apart, to figure out who they were: Jewish or Christian? What did they like to eat? I thought if you ate fish and vegetables, you were probably shy. If you liked to have a glass of cold milk with a peanut-butter-and-jelly sandwich, you were probably outgoing. If you really loved chocolate-chip cookies and held them under the water to soften them, then mashed them up in a bowl to eat, you were an artist. Being female meant you were more aware of these differences.

In the second grade at McDowell Elementary School, I tried out for the softball team, which was all boys. I certainly couldn't hit as hard as a guy, but I got on because I could throw really far. There was one Afro-American boy, Peter Streeter, who was my close friend. The other boys on the team didn't really want me to play, so Peter beat one of them up. From then on, it was okay that I was on the team. I knew boys could intimidate me or protect me. There were also times in my life when no one stood up for me. That doesn't mean I didn't stand up for myself. I would visualize a powerful king or queen inside my chest and I could become very scary.

This visualization also worked for me in my early twenties. I lived in a dangerous neighborhood called Hell's Kitchen. Coming home alone at two o'clock in the morning to my neighborhood, friends would ask if I was afraid. I wasn't. I feel like I can be as strong as I need to be. I have been physically attacked and, to my surprise, I beat the guy up. I was crazed that anyone would put their hands on me. I felt the power of my sister who I watched beat up a boy who had slapped me. I was about seven years old. Maybe seeing her do it when I was so little gave me that crazy confidence. The power to pull out a part of you that has never showed itself before, worked in other parts of my life as well. I was able to direct a network TV rock and roll show in the early '70s because of it. I just acted "as if" I knew what I was doing and I got the job! This got me into the DGA (Directors Guild of America). There were very few women directors, and I was the youngest member. When I worked on a show, I always wore very high platform shoes and long pants so that I would have a more commanding presence. I'd walk in for a preproduction meeting with a group of men who were twenty years older than me. I wanted to look down on them. I grew tired of my shoes, my games, my trying to win respect, and stopped directing so that I could concentrate on photography. This field seemed simpler to me. No meetings where I constantly had to prove myself. My photographs would be my proof of who I was and my abilities. This was the mid-1970s and I thought that instead of directing ABC's *In Concert*, I could just make photographs and sell them to the record labels. At that time in the music business there were no women executives, but there were publicists. There were also very few women pop or rock artists: Joni Mitchell, Carly Simon, Patti Smith, to name a few. Women singers weren't played on the radio in anywhere near the numbers that men were. It was hard for women to be taken seriously, particularly in terms of equal pay with men who were doing the same job. I didn't mind. I could earn a living with photography and feel free to be who I was; I didn't have crews. I could do things on my own. Fortunately, most artists knew that what they wanted were images of themselves that made them look good and promoted what their music was about. It didn't matter what gender I was; it mattered what I could bring to the table to help their career. Artists were always helpful to me.

In the beginning, I did a lot of concert work, but I never wanted to be on the road doing the same thing every day. I thought it was boring. You have the same people around you all the time, and they think that their world is the whole world. As much as I photographed musicians, I stretched out and covered other kinds of subject matter: sports figures, authors, actors, politicians, and also people who were not in the limelight. The camera was a passport into all different kinds of universes. I felt incredibly lucky that this tool provided me with the opportunity to become intensely involved with wherever I was and whomever I was with. When it was over, I could move on to a new learning experience. I could, as my mother suggested, "Live, Live, Live!"

Looking back, I've tried to break limiting thought patterns all my life. Being female is a fact. However, it didn't mean that because of my gender I should become a schoolteacher or get married or have children. That might be right for some people, but I didn't feel it was what I wanted. Thinking of yourself in terms of how the world expects you to be is as frivolous as thinking that your religion or your skin color dictates what you can or cannot do. A person is either male or female, and that has an effect on how you are perceived. So does being fat or thin, beautiful or unattractive, rich or poor, white or black or in between. It's important to acknowledge what it all means when wrapped together with your spirit.

I used to think about this as a kid: If I died and could come back, what would I want to come back as, a man or a woman? There are struggles in being either. That's life. So, if I got to pick, I'd want to grow up female!

Lynn Goldsmith

Joyce Carol Oates

Joyce Carol Oates was born and raised in rural western New York. Grade school was a one-room schoolhouse. She attended Syracuse University on scholarship, graduating as valedictorian, and earned an M.A. in English at the University of Wisconsin. She has devoted her life to teaching and writing, producing more than seventy books including novels, short-story collections, poetry volumes, plays, literary criticism, and essays. She received the National Book Award for her novel them *(1969), the Rosenthal Award from the American Academy–Institute of Arts and Letters, a Guggenheim Fellowship, the O. Henry Prize for Continued Achievement in the Short Story, the Elmer Holmes Bobst Lifetime Achievement Award in Fiction, the Rea Award for the Short Story, and, in 1978, membership in the American Academy Institute.*

IT WAS AN ERA WHEN SUCH WORDS as "sex" and "sexual" were never uttered, even by those who routinely engaged in sexual practices. "Sexy" was a word that might be murmured in an undertone, with a sly movement of the eyes, a knowing smile.

Mrs. Thayer, as housemother to our sorority, had the delicate task of alluding to certain things without ever naming them. Like most housemothers of the day, she spoke of ladylike behavior at all times, standards of decorum, and maintaining a reputation beyond reproach. She used such expressions as "male visitor" and "male person," as if speaking of a distasteful and untrustworthy species. You would not have believed that Agnes Thayer had ever been married, despite the conspicuous rings she wore on her left hand; you would not have believed that this woman had been married to any "male person." Mrs. Thayer lectured us at mealtimes and at formal house meetings (not Kappa ritual meetings) held on Sunday evenings in the parlor. "Our house rules regarding male persons are simple. They are set by the dean of women, and they are not to be violated under any circumstances." It was forbidden to allow any "male person" (other than an approved workman) to ascend to the upper floors of the house; it was forbidden, in fact, to allow any "male person" to sit on the first few steps of the sweeping staircase to the second floor or to enter the basement stairway for any purpose whatsoever. Of course it was forbidden to hide, or to attempt to hide, any "male person" on the premises before or after the house was officially locked for the night; it was forbidden to "carry on" in any manner unbecoming a lady with any "male person" in any of the public rooms or elsewhere technically under Mrs. Thayer's jurisdiction. In the public rooms of the Kappa house, where "male persons" were admitted as guests, the rule was classic in its simplicity: "*All feet* on the floor, girls, *at all times*."

Mrs. Thayer's arch, overbearing accent made her speech irresistible to mimic. In this way, her speech pervaded every room of the thirty-bedroom house.

You thought of sex continuously. Even if, like me, you had few sexual feelings and no desire to translate those feelings into relationships with "male persons." Sex was a tide, vast and virulent and unspeakable. A tide that could wash over any girl at any time, and destroy us. "Male persons" were primed to discharge this tide, in hot little spurts: *semen*. (Yet "semen" was never named.) "Male persons" were the natural predators of *girls*.

"What Thayer's scared of, like all housemothers," it was remarked slightingly of our vigilant housemother, "is one of us getting knocked up. She figures she'd be blamed, and fired."

Forbidden for undergraduate girls to ascend to the upper floors of male residences or to slip from their public rooms at any time. *Forbidden for undergraduate girls* to visit the rooms or apartments of men living off campus and therefore not under the jurisdiction of any university authority. It was especially crucial for girls to avoid being alone with one or more "male persons" at fraternity parties, where unfortunate incidents were rumored to occur occasionally. When a girl drank too much and became careless. Got passed around upstairs, from "date" to "date." But there were no male equivalents of housemothers like Mrs. Thayer at fraternities, only house managers or advisers, and when Kappa girls went to fraternity parties on campus or at Cornell, as they did every weekend, they did as they pleased. Or as their dates pleased.

C'mon! You'll like this guy. He's a great guy. You can't be working all the time! I made up my face like the other faces, I brushed my snarled hair till it shone. I was given a pink taffeta dress to wear, a skirt to midcalf, and a big bow tied at my back to make the waist fit. I was given sparkly earrings. Smiling and blinking like a nocturnal animal prodded out into the sunshine. In the fraternity house, the din was deafening. The young men, en masse, were *tall*. Laughter, music. Beer. Paper cups, beer. The sacrament was beer. In the restroom reserved for LADIES (a poster in smeary red paint taped to the outside of the door), there was a giant blue box of Kotex prominently in view. Some wag had put, in each of the toilets, goldfish. Were you supposed to laugh? Flush the beautiful golden little fish down the toilet and laugh? I lacked an appropriate sense of humor, I lacked an appreciation of beer. And mouths tasting of beer. Was I expected to dance in this din, in a crush of grinning strangers, in a grinding embrace? Expected to kiss a stranger? Some boy who didn't know me, had forgotten my name? What was the purpose of drinking to get drunk? My Kappa sister Chris, vomiting off the back steps onto garbage cans marked ΦΩ. *Chris, come on. Chris, please.* I was begging, but she refused to listen. Back to the party! I was trying to explain to Dawn, Jill, Donna, Trudi, who were impatient with me, eyes hotly shining, skin heated, arms slung around their grinning dates' necks. *She'll be fine, Chris can take care of herself. She's been at these parties before.* I provoked embarrassment and disgust among those Kappas sober enough to notice how I left drunken Eddy, my "date," walking out of the music blare and running across the snowy, spiky-grassed park in ridiculously high heels, my borrowed pink taffeta dress swishing like ice against my stockinged legs, breathless, cursing, tears leaking out of my eyes, though goddamn I wasn't crying, why cry? *My feelings can't be hurt where I have none.*

Next day around noon, Trudi, looking coarse-faced and homely without makeup, brought the black cloth coat I'd left on the crammed coatrack at the fraternity house, tossed it onto my bed with a look of pity and contempt. "Here, you forgot something."

What happened to Chris?

Hey if she doesn't remember, so what?

Whose business? Yours?

No memory, nothing to forgive.

Her date took precautions, probably. He isn't a complete ass-hole.

Was it just him?

Joyce Carol Oates

Heidi Kuhn

Heidi Kuhn is the founder and president of Roots of Peace, whose goal is to remove land mines from affected countries and return the land to agricultural use. She worked in the field of international business management for American Express and Barclays Bank, then opened a television media company in Alaska. She later started NewsLink International, where she developed global communications and social-justice stories for the media. She is a graduate of the University of California at Berkeley in political economics of industrial societies, and she received the 2003 UC Berkeley Alumni of the Year Award for Excellence and Achievement.

November 1963

THE INSPIRATION TO PLANT the roots of peace on earth is deeply embedded in my childhood. On a cold November day at Dominican Garden School in San Rafael, California, I vividly remember coloring pictures with my best friend, Michael Pelfini, as the rain gently fell outside the window.

Suddenly our parents rushed into the room with tears streaming down their faces. They were scrambling to put our raincoats on us, and I remember being very confused as to whether this effort was to protect us from the rain outside or the flood of tears flowing down their faces.

I exchanged parting glances with Michael, for our colorful pictures were now overshadowed by clouds of gray and black. No words, just tears. As I prepared to leave, holding my mother's gentle hand, I looked into the face of my beloved teacher, Sister Patricia, and asked her what I could do to help make all the mommies and daddies stop crying. She quietly answered, "Go home, and pray for peace with all of your heart, for our dear President John F. Kennedy was just assassinated."

That evening, I prayed and prayed with the innocence and heart of a five-year-old child.

After I fell asleep, I vividly remember awakening with the presence of a heavenly being in my room. I opened my eyes to see the most beautiful woman I had ever seen, standing to the right of my bed with her arms outstretched. I was not afraid, but only comforted by the warmth of spirit that filled the room. Instinctively I got out of my bed and knelt down before her. Her face was pale and translucent, with light and love that emanated from within.

She spoke to me and asked me to fulfill an important promise. I remember responding with sincere reverence and respect—promising deeply to fulfill what was asked of me. The transference of golden light extended from the palms of her hands and radiated into my being. My inner soul vowed to keep a very deep promise made and never to be forgotten.

My dear mother remembers my waking her up and going on and on about the vision. She stayed up most of the night reassuring me that it was only a dream. I was insistent that it was a real experience and that there was a special message to share.

The following morning, I begged my mother to take me to St. Raphael's Mission church—named for the angel of healing. While my mother was extremely tired, she put on her red Pendleton suit with matching red hat and took me to church. I held her hand, deeply praying to the beautiful lady that visited my bedroom.

Years passed, and the spirit of the Blessed Mother has never left me. It was there in the former Soviet Union when I gave hundreds of blue plastic rosary beads to Metropolitan Pitirim—a leader of the Russian Orthodox Church. Unknown to me was the fact that each rosary had the prayer from Our Lady of Fatima—when the Blessed Mother appeared to a group of children in Portugal in 1912—laminated as an attachment which prayed for the conversion of Russia. The Blessed Mother was there at my bedside as I was wheeled into surgery for malignant cervical cancer, eight years before I gave birth to a little son named Christian. She was there in the first month of the new millennium as I visited Zagreb, Croatia, on a U.S. Department of State tour to the minefields. The stunning statue of the Blessed Mother in the heart of Zagreb reminds me of the vision—it is one of the only representations I have ever seen that reminds me of the spirit of that very special dream. Finally she was there when Croatian-born Mike Grgich, owner of Grgich Hills Winery, in Napa Valley, California, wrapped some simple grape cuttings to be planted in his homeland. There we were led to the site of Mary in Medjugorje, where her message to the children was, "Peace, peace, only peace." The roots of peace were planted beneath the site of the vision of Mary.

Recently I traveled to Afghanistan with the ABC local news anchor Cheryl Jennings and my teenage daughter, Kyleigh. Together we went as three women walking in the name of peace, a miracle in its own right. Following 9/11, Roots of Peace raised the necessary funds to remove landmines north of Kabul in the once fertile Shomali Plains. Removing over a hundred thousand land mines and UXOs (unexploded ordnances) near Baghram Air Force Base, our group then planted grapevines. Although the Muslim culture does not permit the consumption of wine, we trained over three thousand Afghan farmers to plant grapes on former minefields. Later we visited them in their fields to witness the harvest of hope—eight hundred tons of grapes.

As they pulled out their Muslim beads, I also pulled out my rosary beads. We joined hands praying to the same God for peace in the vineyards. Later the Afghan farmers told me of a chapter in the Koran about the Blessed Mother Mary and her prayers for peace. It was at this moment that I realized my childhood dream.

Heidi Kühn

Lisa Gay Hamilton

*Interested in the theatre from an early age, LisaGay Hamilton took
private acting lessons in middle school and spent her summers in
drama camps. Her primary interest was Shakespearean theatre. She
graduated in drama from New York University and went on to graduate from Juilliard's Drama Division. From 1997 to 2003, she was a
regular on the TV series* The Practice. *She has appeared in a number of movies, including* True Crime, Beloved, The Truth About
Charlie, *and* Nine Lives. *While working on* Beloved, *she met the
African American actress Beah Richards. Inspired by Richards's story
of her life in the theatre and as a political activist, Hamilton wrote, directed, and coproduced the documentary* Beah: A Black Woman
Speaks.

GROWING UP FEMALE IS A JOURNEY.

When I think about what it means to "grow up female," I
cannot separate my gender from my race or any of my many
identities. At forty, I learned the most valuable lesson of my entire life: the key to true freedom is self-love. Self-love means
embracing all the parts of myself—woman, African American,
mother, sister, daughter, partner, artist, and parts yet to be de-

veloped. The combination of all of our identities is what makes us whole, what makes us human. By "human" I don't mean to suggest that we should overlook color or gender or the differences that make us unique. Instead, we need to see one another in all of our complexity and appreciate our different histories and experiences.

I look at my parents and the era they lived through and appreciate my own upbringing. They lived in Jim Crow Mississippi and Alabama. For black people confronting that level of racism, we had no choice but to find ways to love ourselves. It was necessary for our survival as a people. Looking back, I can see now how my parents instilled in my sister and me that sense of pride and self-love.

Both of my parents worked. My grandmother, who lived with us, took care of me during the day. I've always loved older people, perhaps because my first friend was my grandmother. We spent a great deal of time alone together, and she always seemed very focused on me. She complimented me and really stimulated my imagination by joining me in tea parties and dress-up with my dolls and stuffed animals. That was an incredibly rich experience. I was eight years old when she died.

Coming from a household of very strong women, I think the way I discovered how to be heard was through "pretend," through storytelling. I loved to sing, in particular African American musicals, as well as jazz, and I would lip-synch to artists like Nina Simone when I was five years old.

I believe in the power of storytelling. It can inspire. It can entertain as well as move you and make you think. Untruthful stories are dangerous. I remember being fed myths in the classroom, being taught, for example, how enslaved Africans were docile and happy in their bondage. My mother stormed into my classroom on numerous occasions demanding that the truth be told. I remember one instance when she stormed into metal shop to battle the myth that shop class was for boys only. Although my mother succeeded in getting me into the class, I was never allowed to use the equipment. I was this lone black girl surrounded by white boys wearing goggles and wielding torches while I sat there watching the teacher make all of my projects. By the way, I got an A in the class.

After being accepted into the Juilliard Drama Division, a white woman from the Financial Aid office remarked, "Perhaps you would be happier somewhere else." She said this *after* I was accepted and awarded a full scholarship. When I graduated, I was the only black person in my class. Toward the end of the year, we had auditions in front of a sea of agents and directors, and I knew that no one was going to call me. Sure enough, I was right. The big agencies approached most of my female classmates while I was ignored. I never had any misgivings, however, because I knew that my journey would be different.

Throughout my career, I've had to grapple with Hollywood's misrepresentations of black women, not to mention the limited number of roles available to women of color. We are essentially invisible. Most of the time I find myself refusing certain roles because they are demeaning. In making these choices, I've had to make significant sacrifices professionally and financially. Yet, I would not have it any other way. I'm proud of the choices I've made.

I've often felt very alone in an industry that peddles falsehoods. Then I met Beah Richards, an actress, poet, and social activist, who committed her life to telling the truth no matter the consequences. She paved the way for artists like me, always remaining principled in her struggle to overturn myths about women and people of color. She taught me the importance of finding the true meaning of words. Knowing the definition and history of words changes everything. Truth empowers you. Telling the truth in a creative way is my calling. As Beah taught me, our charge as actors, or as human beings for that matter, is truth-telling. This is precisely the power of the craft, our ability and obligation as artists to "capture the conscience of the King."

I would like to share with all women the gift Beah gave me—the definition of the word "being." Being is mortal existence in a complete and perfect state, lacking no essential characteristic, perfect, God. This definition frees us from, as Beah would say, "all the chains and things that bind your mind and your body." This definition of being says that who you are in this moment is perfect—not perfect in the sense that there is nothing to improve upon. Perfect in the African sense of being in motion, evolving, moving toward that which is divine. This definition enabled me to see myself, to love myself as a whole person—an evolving yet unrealized human being. Giving our young girls that truthful definition allows them to walk much taller and have the capacity to love others more, because they love themselves. We are humanity. We bring forth life. We are the nurturers. We are the caregivers. These are roles to be treasured because we're perfect.

LisaGay Hamilton

Sally Fisher

Sally Fisher is a cofounder of Northern Lights Alternatives, a network of HIV/AIDS support agencies. Her book Life Mastery *(1993) is based on her experiences and workshops. Healing meditations are included in her audiocassettes* Spirituality: Insight and Meditation *and* Burnout Prevention and Recovery: Getting Life Back on Track.

As I waited on the La Guardia Airport tarmac, heading for Santa Fe, New Mexico, my mind wandered to, among other things, what I had to say about being born female. I had stowed my computer for liftoff, glanced around the cabin to check out my fellow travelers, and I swear this happened: A man across the aisle snapped opened his newspaper to expose an article with the following boldface: "Soon we will be able to choose the sex of our children, but should we?" I'm no longer sure of the exact wording, but the drift is as clear as its implication. Let me put it this way: If it had been possible to do such a thing before I was conceived, there would be one less vagina in this world today.

They say that we teach what we need to learn. By the same

token, I think that we are each attracted to certain causes, certain work that ignites our spirit and brings with it not just lessons but the potential for our own healing. So many women need healing from nothing more than being disenfranchised, undervalued, and born female.

My work puts me smack in the middle of a world where female fetuses are aborted and where far too many of those who pop from the womb fully formed and ready for life encounter struggles that seldom befall male children.

I didn't get involved in my work because my life physically resembled any of these women's; in fact, I grew up with a silver spoon in my mouth, and no one ever laid a hand on me. Yet there was a dark underbelly, which included the idea that neither parent really valued girls, each for his or her own reasons. It was a time when girls were expected to marry, have children, and replicate the lives of their mothers. I was not expected to become someone of value on my own, to accomplish amazing things or challenge the status quo. The measure of my worth was related to snagging the right guy and having a socially appropriate life.

When I reached my teens, my mom and I had a little heart-to-heart. She said that she was glad I had girlfriends but that I should be careful. I shouldn't completely trust them. They might give me false compliments or give me advice about what to wear without my best interests in mind and then steal my boyfriends, my currency in the world. Hmmm, not trust girls. *I* was a girl. If she was right, then could I even trust myself? Always questioning, I decided to find another way to think about girls.

I began to look for women I could use as role models. I had been born too late for Eleanor Roosevelt, and neither Bess Truman nor Mamie Eisenhower measured up to what I longed for. Probably one of the greatest female influences on my childhood and closest to a role model was a warm, strong, and loving live-in housekeeper named Ethel. I would sit in her room in the afternoons with my paper and crayons all over the floor, listening to radio. We listened to *Let's Pretend* and *News at Noon* or *The Nightly News*. Ethel explained the things I didn't understand. I developed an equal love for fantasy and reality, and my girlhood affair with the radio left me longing for romance, feeling every slight to the downtrodden, and wanting to right every wrong. And then I discovered comic books and Wonder Woman. Wonder Woman had it all. She was beautiful. She had a tiny waist, was almost invincible, but most important she was a woman out to save the world. She did what only men were supposed to do. It never occurred to me that there was a real downside to being an Amazon stuck on earth without community, living in the necessary fiction of being less than she really was while expected to be on call 24/7 to do the impossible. Nonetheless, I longed to be her.

Longing was my predominant emotion as a kid. Longing to be seen, to be taken seriously, to prove that I could do what the guys could do, to feel less of the world's suffering, to be given the credit I deserved for being smart, caring, and capable. I longed to be rid of the doubts that I'd accumulated about girls, about myself. Were women trustworthy? Were we as valuable as boys, as men?

I maintained my intention to right society's wrongs, to be a Wonder Woman. My parents told me that I couldn't save the world, that I was overreaching, and that there were men in high places doing those things. Oh, really? I formed myself in almost complete opposition to their every belief, value, position, and hope. But somehow, my rebellion notwithstanding, I found myself caught in a trap of my own making. No matter how much I wanted to strike out on my own, reinvent myself, and change society, I desperately wanted to be loved, accepted, approved of, and appreciated by these parents who thought my femaleness could be solved only by marriage.

This began to play itself out as I left the girl behind and became a woman. I plunged into activism, still wanting to save the world, but at the same time I found that I was waiting to be saved. And I was. I married a man who saved me from having to figure out how to make a life on my own, something for which I had no training. Sadly, in being saved I gave away some of the best parts of myself. We imitated my parents' life, the one they'd envisioned for me but nearly drove me mad, until I couldn't do it anymore and until I began to get a sense that I really was a wonder and a really good woman. Evidence flew in the face of my mother's story about women. Women were in fact amazing, a message I instilled in my own daughters and in my son.

Since that time, I have indeed made a life and do my best to save the world. I've worked in the arts, been in the AIDS movement, founded an international AIDS agency, and sought to end violence against women and girls. I've created an international organization that catalyzes coalitions among the women's movement, those working in HIV/AIDS, and those working in related fields, primarily in Africa and India. When I see their magnificence and my own daughters' magnificence and see the spirit of possibility in these women—their spirit to carry on under impossible circumstances—I see my own reflection in their eyes and know that if they are divine, so are all women, including me, and so was my mother, who never had a "sister" extend her the hand of hope to help her see herself.

I have learned that women are warriors who need no weapons, who can love and redefine the paradigms of war and peace, who can disarm an enemy with an embrace. Women know that food, compassion, and understanding are more powerful than bullets, bombs, and blockades. Women understand that our own wounds, from the skinned knees and scraped elbows of childhood to the broken hearts of romance to the deep wounds of abuse and longing, can all be healed and beckon us to walk the road toward our magnificent, extraordinary, divine women selves. The payoff for being born female.

Sally Fisher

Carol Channing

Tony Award winner Channing is celebrated for her roles in two Broad-way hit shows: as Lorelei in the 1950s Gentlemen Prefer Blondes *and as Dolly Gallagher Levi in* Hello, Dolly! *(1964). Her perfor-mance in the film* Thoroughly Modern Millie *(1967) brought her a Golden Globe and an Oscar nomination. In 2003, the eighty-two-year-old Channing married her former high-school sweetheart, Harry Kullijian.*

"IT'S AMAZING YOU'RE STILL ALIVE," my cousin Dickie tells me. That's because when I was only a few weeks old, my mother told him he had to help look after me. At the time, we lived in Seattle, where my father was city editor of the *Seattle Star*. Dickie would tie my baby buggy onto the back of his tri-cycle and we'd go on death trips—terrible, wild, dangerous trips through Seattle. He would drag me around, and the baby buggy would almost fall over.

I was still in a crib when I started imitating people, starting with my Uncle Belinore. He had loose teeth, and I remember thinking, *Uncle Belinore thurtainly has trouble with thomething.* And

I would say words that sounded like him to myself and laugh because it did sound like him.

When I was in grammar school, I found every excuse to go to the principal's office just to hear her talk. Miss Barrard, in the way she spoke, was a forerunner of Julia Child. When I would have tea parties with imaginary friends—I really enjoyed being alone with all those imaginary people—I'd imagine Miss Barrard saying, "We've got to clean up the yard," then Mr. Schwartz, a teacher, saying, "Well, I don't know." And I would go over these conversations and laugh at what I made up for Miss Barrard and Mr. Schwartz to say. I'd think, *Oh, that's why it was funny, because he said it that way.* I think it was because I was an only child. If I had brothers and sisters, I wouldn't have been alone enough to think about it. These were always real people, somebody who was absolutely fascinating to me. There was a Miss Weaver, who was fascinating because she had a Bronx accent. I had never heard a Bronx accent before, so I thought she was terrific.

The fondest memories I have of my childhood are the three years I went together with a boy named Harry (now he's my husband!) in the seventh, eighth, and ninth grades. He was the leader of the school band, and I thought he was the most beautiful thing I had ever seen. He was the captain of the soccer team, and we won the California championship because of him. We went everywhere together, to the opera house where I used to be a super in the ballet. They chose Harry instead of me to be in *Aida* as part of the army. He looked just right—they didn't even have to make him up. At that age, he looked like he came from the Holy Land.

This is the world. This is the way it always is going to be, I thought. I'd wake up happy. I'd see Harry at school, and he would take me home. Then I found out that life isn't like that at all. You go through terrible things, which is the only way we grow. Otherwise, we don't learn anything. Looking back, I realize how important it is to be miserable at a certain time and to overcome challenges. Now those happy years are back, and I don't care if I ever work again.

After Seattle, we moved to my grandmother's house in San Francisco. I was very cautious. I think it was because I was nearsighted but didn't know it. I could fall into the nearest open manhole at any moment, so I always kind of slid around with my feet first to see where I was going. But once people got within my view, where I could see them, it was such news—here were human beings, and look at them! It thrilled me. I remember every expression on their faces.

My grandmother was crazy about movies, so we would go to see the silent films of that time. I've been going to movies my entire life. Movies are particularly American; if they're not, they don't sell. As a child, I knew what movies everybody considered terrific, and I loved them. Girls know what glamour is—they don't know what sex appeal is, but they know what glamour is. They can sense it is attractive to the opposite sex, and it reminds a little girl that it's fun to be a girl. Clara Bow had such glamour. I wrote her a fan letter and am still waiting to this day to get an answer.

We went to the movies before I even went to kindergarten, so I knew all about the Charleston and the Black Bottom. It's very strange, really, that I knew all that and used it later, so you see there's no wasted time in any of our lives. All of a sudden, it turned up when I was doing the play *Lend an Ear*. Everybody in the cast was the same age, but I knew those dances because I went to all the movies starring Dorothy Mackaill and Jack Mulhall. I knew every step. The company wanted to know how I knew. While I was sitting in a movie theater, the rest of them were reading *Mrs. Wiggs of the Cabbage Patch*, and all kinds of lovely English things like *Oliver Twist*. But that's not a reflection of our society. Why do they make children read something that has nothing to do with their lives?

When I was six, we saw *Gentlemen Prefer Blondes*, and I kept imitating Ruth Taylor, the girl who played in it. I loved her new boyish bob that the flappers had and tried the haircut out on my grandmother first. Unfortunately, one side somehow ended up longer than the other and the bangs were too short. It took about six months for her hair to grow out—I should have tried it out on myself first. I also made my grandmother up like Jean Harlow, who had funny hooks on top of her eyes for eyebrows. Grandmothers let you do things like that. After my handiwork, my grandmother looked like she was always asking a question; one side of her eyebrows was curved and the other flat, as if she were asking, "Why? What is that?" Before we'd leave for church, I'd place water-wave combs in her hair, give her a cupid's-bow mouth, and brush lavender and blue shadow on her lids. As I came up from Sunday school, people would ask me, "What happened to your grandmother? She run into something?" But she would just walk around that way, letting me do anything I wanted.

We saw the movie about Rear Admiral Richard Evelyn Byrd and his trip to the South Pole seven different times. Seven different Saturdays. We would get a Horlicks malted milk between movies. There was one movie that Kay Francis was in, a silent film named *Illusion*, and on top of the box office there was a sign saying No Children Allowed. My grandmother and I just walked up and she said, "Two, please." They didn't stop us, and I saw the whole thing. For most of the movie, Kay Francis was sitting in a bathtub, and all I thought was, *Why is she sitting in a bathtub? To get clean?* I don't think children understand what's going on in those situations. Once I was on a plane with my son, Chan, and we were watching *Splendor in the Grass*. I said, "Chan, I have to go to the lavatory. Tell me what happened when I get back. I don't want to miss a thing." When I came back, he said, "You didn't miss a thing—just the boy and the girl were on the bed wrestling."

Growing up, I never saw any black people. When I was sixteen, my mother told me I had African-American blood. My father's mother was black. There's a picture, now lost, of my grandmother that I saw as a child. "Why is she in the dark?" I asked. "Well, the light wasn't on her," they told me. My mother thought the news of my having African-American blood would just slay me. But knowing I have that in my heritage never bothered me. The joke was that I thought, *How wonderful.* Nine years ago, I found out that my mother was Jewish. So I have the two greatest strains in show business running through me. I've been celebrating ever since I found out.

Carol Channing

Taina Bien-Aimé

Taina Bien-Aimé is the executive director of Equality Now, an international human-rights organization whose main concern is the protection and promotion of women's rights. The organization documents violence and discrimination against women and initiates actions to advance equal rights and defend individual women who suffer abuse. Issues of concern include domestic violence, rape, female genital mutilation, denial of reproductive rights, sex trafficking, women's political participation, and equal access to education and employment. She holds a Juris Doctor from New York University School of Law and a licence in political science from the University of Geneva/Graduate School of International Studies, Switzerland.

LIKE MY MOTHER AND GRANDMOTHER and their grandmothers before them, I am a firstborn daughter, progeny of a long line of women with strong spines and a legendary low tolerance for nonsense. My first duty in life was to remember that.

The journey that led to my life's work—defending the human rights of women and girls around the world at Equality Now—began at the kitchen table, where women kin gathered

at the end of long weeks of wearisome workplaces and testing husbands. They had trickled to the shores of New York
from Haiti, the first wave of the Papa Doc Duvalier escapees,
a murderous time when mulattoes were the first to be punished by death for their fair-skinned arrogance and schizo-
phrenic love of their Napoleonic heritage. They fled a
suffocating paradise where girls could not ride bicycles for
fear they would stray from the nest they rarely left before
their wedding day.

The kitchen table replaced the wooden porches perched
in the shadows of the Carib sun, where womenfolk sipped
fruit punch on wicker rocking chairs, welcoming fresh gos-
sip from the neighborhood. My first understanding of love
began at the kitchen table in their new world, where kisses
and suffocating hugs under perfumed breath greeted any
small child walking by to request milk or to whine. I nestled
in the folds of these muses, whose hues reflected centuries
of colonialism and the brutal import of African blood, de-
scendants of a native tribe whose name I bear.

For fear of being shushed away with the other children,
I learned to observe around the kitchen table in silence, until my presence was forgotten. I focused on these women's
rhythms as they rolled dough for pâtés or set curlers in a
friend's hair, their singsong voices interlaced with laughter
and raw jokes. I was enchanted by the swaying of their hips,
the easy smiles, and the sucking clicks their mouths made
emphasizing edicts my young ears could not at first grasp.
My early orb was one of magical and fearless women, Creole

earrings and red lipsticks, matriarchs of my soul, who deliberated life with authority and conviction. Those afternoons, my father, whose devotion was deep despite his quiet presence, would often wink at me, sipping espresso against a counter far from the kitchen table, futilely waiting for me to escape for a merengue lesson or a mean game of Monopoly.

But I belonged to my mother. She led the chorus that cursed the Virgin Mary for blessing them with no choice but to worship her holy virtue and embrace the sacrifices her church demanded of our gender. She wanted me to hear mesmerizing tales and secrets woven around the kitchen table that taught a young girl the beauty and pain of being female.

Slowly, in time measured by seasons, I began to decode whispers of marital infidelities or tips on how to tackle unwanted touches from lewd bosses. The kitchen table converted into my training ground to crystallize images of strength and oppression, defiance and despair, as I realized that my elders struggled for a freedom they could neither define nor grasp. When a black eye occasionally appeared at the kitchen table despite admonitions to leave the louse once and for all, my mother joined the collective disdain and impatience. If you had no power, damn it, you could at least show pride and not flaunt weakness in public. I would watch that bruised woman, wanting to touch the frail loneliness, since I knew that years would pass before she would return to share her sorrow. My mother would instead glare at me, a warning against bad marriages and feeble women. On the eve of puberty, the truth about my devoted Caribbean warriors began unraveling. The sanctified fiefdom of the kitchen table was an illusion in which I could no longer bask. My matriarchs ruled only within these corners, their hearts cursing sparse conjugal love while upbeat island tempos drowned the sorrows of their deceived lives.

I came of age in the seventies, when feminism was the talk of the town and political demonstrations overwhelmed the evening news. My mother reminded me, as she dabbed Vaseline on my unruly eyebrows, never to depend on a man. She handed me the first issue of *Ms.* magazine, with a plea to look into her eyes and avoid the missteps of her life. I gave up competing with my coquettish cousins, who flocked to grooming salons, and signed up for boarding school, where girls from countries near and far shared their own kitchen-table stories of wonder. My quest to discover why the first woman on earth had failed to reclaim the serpent's theft drove me to Simone de Beauvoir's *Second Sex* and Sojourner Truth's writings, Susan Brownmiller's *Against Our Will: Men, Women and Rape*, Robin Morgan's *Sisterhood Is Powerful*, and the French classics that punished their heroines for seizing the freedoms they believed theirs by birth. This journey eventually led me to law school, where I learned how the institutionalization of violence and discrimination across centuries and continents barely matched the tireless efforts that challenged such abuses.

Years later, as I watched breast cancer devour my mother whole, my first child flipping in my womb, her eyes betrayed disappointment. She had hoped her daughters would have saved her from the kitchen table she so despised, not understanding that love and kindness would never be enough to defeat forces of oppression. Even through her admiration of Equality Now, a unique place where promoting the rights of women often gets accomplished through effective advocacy, her gaze questioned where I had failed. She should have known that every day unspeakable horrors against women and girls unfold before our eyes and clash with the courage and rage of unsung heroes amid the rubble as they envision a future where dignity and safety prevail. She should have known that our climb toward justice rests on countless shoulders on which we each tiptoe, trying to reach the rainbow's arc, and that no lifetime has ever seen a thousand rainbows. At the edge of water, long ago, she had discarded the kitchen table, its memories of love and fury still lingering closer to hope than to desolation. We were saying good-bye, neither of us knowing that the long line of firstborn daughters would end with my beloved sons, but that myriad little girls, nourished at kitchen tables in unexpected corners of the world, would watch their mothers on the horizon, inviting them to join the long quest toward equality, perhaps in quiet ways, but always miraculous.

Taina Bien-Aimé

Marlee Matlin

Marlee Beth Matlin, the third child born to parents Don and Libby Matlin, of Morton Grove, Illinois, was rendered deaf at the age of eighteen months after a bout with roseola infantum. She acted throughout her childhood, and this early interest in drama continued after she'd graduated with a degree in criminal justice from Harper College in Illinois. A role in a stage production of the play Children of a Lesser God *led to a reprise of that role in the film version, for which she received the Academy Award for Best Actress. She has gone on to act in many films and television shows. She also has her own production company, Solo One.*

AS A YOUNG JEWISH GIRL growing up hearing-impaired, I was fortunate that I was born into a family that never took no for an answer. Some called it guts, some called it empowerment. I called it chutzpah. My family never let my deafness stand in my way.

That's not to say growing up was easy, despite the fact that my family was so single-minded. Sometimes I experienced frustration and sometimes I failed, but that was part of growing up. Every day was about opening that front door and exploring that neighborhood on my own. In the end, I grew up in a manner that was secure and challenging, enabled and respectful. I had a bat mitzvah, the female version of a Jewish rite of passage traditionally afforded to young boys but which grew to include young girls as well. In my case, it was a rite of passage that was crucial to my understanding of the importance of inclusion and empowerment, particularly of young women.

I began my studies in earnest, with a rabbi who both signed and spoke. Every day I worked to phonetically pronounce the Hebrew that would eventually be part of my haftarah, the text from Prophets read in the synagogue on Sabbath mornings. By the time my bat mitzvah day had arrived, I was ready to show the world I could accomplish anything, despite the predictions to the contrary.

As I read my portion, I looked out to the audience for inspiration. But instead of smiling faces, I saw my mother and father crying. Naturally I started crying too; I didn't know the difference between tears of joy and tears of sadness! Soon everybody was crying. After taking a moment to compose myself, I looked down to continue my haftarah and noticed that I had cried on the torah and stained it with my tears. I was mortified. It took all my strength to finish my portion and take my seat beside my family.

After the service, I ran up to the rabbi and apologized. "I ruined the torah with my tears!" Suddenly those who might have doubted my ability to become a young bat mitzvah seemed all too correct.

Just then, the rabbi did something that has stayed with

me ever since. After letting me get it all out, he gently lifted my chin and wiped away my tears. "Marlee," he said, "throughout Jewish history, Jews have shed many tears—tears for those who were persecuted, tears for those who perished. Many times, it was only the stain of tears that served as means to remember and our means to never forget.

"But your tears, Marlee, which we will never forget, are not tears of sadness but tears of joy. Not only are you a young girl entering a circle once reserved only for young men, you are entering as a young girl who happens to be deaf as well. This is an accomplishment that is extraordinary. Your tears will remind us of the achievements you have made as a young girl who is deaf and who has joined the Jewish community. I am proud of your tears and I am proud of you. Don't ever doubt yourself."

So much of the world stands in silence when those less fortunate are shuttled off to dark corners to live out their lives apart from the mainstream. With a lot of help from my parents and a simple rite of passage, I was able to come out from that dark silence and into the light. In the end, I was able to realize that the real handicaps we all experience do not lie in our limbs, eyes, or ears; they lie in our minds. Since then, I have been determined that silence will be the last thing the world ever hears from me.

Martha McPhee

Martha McPhee is the author of the novels L'America, Bright Angel Time, *and* Gorgeous Lies, *which was a National Book Award
finalist in 2002. The recipient of grants from the National Endowment for the Arts and the Guggenheim Foundation, she is also the
coauthor of* Girls: Ordinary Girls and Their Extraordinary Pur-
suits *written with her sisters, Jenny and Laura McPhee. She teaches
at Hofstra University and lives in New York City with her daughter
and her husband, the poet and writer Mark Svenvold.*

I REMEMBER THIS: I'm a little girl. My parents are recently divorced. My mother has all four of her daughters in our study.
She's wearing blue jeans and a T-shirt that reads STAMP OUT SEXISM.
The image on the shirt is of a young girl stomping on a book. My
mother has given us the task of cutting out images from children's
readers, Dick and Jane specifically. We're looking for pictures in
which Jane is passive and Dick is active, in which the mother is described as silly and forgetful, admonished by her businessman husband in his dark suit. She's lost her keys, can't find her gloves, et
cetera. We are looking for images of women in professional roles.
They are mothers, nurses, schoolteachers. Sun streams through the

study windows, and we are hard at work, cutting and noting and showing our mother everything we have found. I am five years old. My sisters' ages ascend from mine, leaping two years per sister. They know what they are doing. I don't really get it, but I do get that my mother is active and happy. After she divorced, she lay in bed for a long time. This project has gotten her out of bed and made her feel she has purpose. She is writing a book with other women who are part of a group called Women on Words and Images. We are involved in the research. My sisters are proud when my mother praises them for finding an image—Dick, say, throwing a ball while Jane watches. The book will come out in a year or so: *Dick and Jane As Victims—Sex Stereotyping in Children's Readers.*

When my mother and father split, my mother did not know how to write a check. The year was 1969. She went to bed and then woke up a while later and got involved. She started working on the books. She opened her own photography studio so that she could provide for her daughters. It soon began to thrive. Her desire more than anything was to give her children a model so that they'd know how to choose for themselves, to understand what it was they dreamed and feel the confidence to pursue it.

I can still feel that sun on my neck in our library. I can see us all working vigorously, understanding and not, but knowing that this was the beginning of something. My mother stands there praising us, the sun caught in her golden hair, her green eyes lit with determination and all that hope.

Martha McPhee

J. K. Rowling

Born in Yate, near Bristol, England, in 1965, Joanne Kathleen
Rowling attended Exeter University, lived in Paris, and later worked
for Amnesty International in London. In 1990, she hit on the idea of
Harry Potter while riding a crowded train from her home in Man-
chester back to London. Over the next five years, she continued to
work on the novel. Divorced and living on public assistance in an un-
heated Edinburgh apartment, she completed Harry Potter and the
Philosopher's Stone *(published as* Harry Potter and the Sor-
cerer's Stone *in the United States) in 1995, writing in a café as her*
infant daughter slept nearby in a stroller. Since the first in the series
was published in 1997, more than a quarter billion Harry Potter
books have been printed. She lives in Scotland with her husband and
three children.

WHEN I WAS YOUNG, I had two teachers whom I found very
inspiring—Pearl Biddle tutored me in French, and Lucy Shep-
herd taught me English. They were passionate pedagogues who
taught me more than their subjects. Pearl was a great believer in
learning for learning's sake, and Lucy was a great role model for
a teenage girl—dry, assertive, and understanding.

When we were growing up, I told my sister, Di, hundreds of stories; she didn't complain too much. We are very close; like many children, we had a dual life, a separate, secret existence apart from my parents. It is now as though we are the only remaining members of an otherwise extinct tribe.

The main female character in the Harry Potter books, Hermione, is drawn largely from my experience of being a young girl. I was very frightened of failure. I've got used to it since, and it doesn't hurt nearly as much as I used to imagine.

I never told my family that I wanted to be a writer. They would have told me I didn't have a hope. People in my family did not become writers. There was a great emphasis on mortgages, pensions, and career paths. I felt I would be taken about as seriously as if I had said I wanted to be a pop star, and sternly dissuaded (not that it would have worked).

I can't think of an occasion when I felt it was useful to be female. I can, however, remember passionately wishing I were a boy on a couple of occasions, but that was because I was dreaming of knocking out a particularly vicious male bully.

The one event that, for me, triggered a deep experience of feminine power is giving birth. There is nothing more magnificent in the whole of nature. Watching my older daughter grow has been very interesting. Some of what she is going through is very familiar—the eternal difficulties of childhood. She is very different from me—an aspiring engineer and a real tomboy—which I love. I am grateful that she is growing up at a time when she can pursue the career

of her choice. She recently read a book about the suffrag-
ettes, and we have been having many dinnertime discussions
about how their various sacrifices led, in the end, to Jessica's
freedom to study technology.

There are many things I liked, then and now, about being
a girl. The friendships you make with other women are very
different from the friendships men make, and I certainly
wouldn't want to swap. I like women's perceptiveness and
ability to empathize. I like their ability to juggle nineteen
jobs before breakfast, and I prefer women's shoes.

Susan Stamberg

Susan Stamberg, special correspondent for NPR, has won virtually every award in broadcasting, including being inducted into both the Broadcasting Hall of Fame and the Radio Hall of Fame. She served as cohost of NPR's award-winning newsmagazine All Things Considered *for fourteen years, hosted* Weekend Edition Sunday, *and now serves as guest host of NPR's* Morning Edition *and* Weekend Edition Saturday, *in addition to reporting on cultural issues for all the NPR programs. A native of New York City, she received a bachelor's degree from Barnard College and has been awarded numerous honorary degrees, including a doctor of humane letters from Dartmouth College. She is a fellow of Silliman College, Yale University, and serves on the boards of the PEN/Faulkner Fiction Award Foundation and Columbia University's Medill School National Arts Journalism Program. She is married to Louis C. Stamberg, and they have one son, Joshua, an actor.*

EVERY GENERATION thinks their era was the most difficult to live through. But I know beyond a doubt that mine was. I grew up in the 1950s, the Age of the Good Girl. We were taught to be sweet, accommodating, polite, agreeable, and not to rock any boats. Also to wear white gloves when we went downtown. And most important for fifties Good Girls, we were expected to get married the moment we finished college, to be supportive, ego-boosting wives, and to raise perfect children.

Graduating in 1959, I was already a failure. I was not engaged. I didn't even have a beau (that's how our mothers referred to our dates). But I'd graduated from Barnard College, a women's school in Manhattan. There we were taught not just to marry and breed after our B.A.'s, we were also expected to have careers that made a difference to society *and* to give something back to our communities. So I was an extremely laden-down fifties Good Girl. Much was expected of me. Still, school had taught me to believe I could meet all expectations. There was nothing I couldn't do. And so did I launch myself into the "real" world.

Daisy Buchanan, the obsession of Jay Gatsby in F. Scott Fitzgerald's *The Great Gatsby*, says about her young daughter, "I'm glad it's a girl. And I hope she'll be a fool—that's the best thing a girl can be in this world, a beautiful little fool." Contrary to all my preparation at Barnard, the idea of women as beautiful fools was very much afloat in the real world when I soared out into young womanhood. And so I prayed that *if* I ever got married, I would not have a daughter. I felt I just wouldn't be able to raise her to conform with the foolish, sometimes simpering things fifties and early-sixties America expected of women. It would be fine if my daughter were beautiful—although I thought society put much too much emphasis on looks.

As far as her being a fool—that's the last thing I wanted for her. So I prayed for a boy. When I finally married Louis Stamberg and had a child, my prayers were answered. This was a baby I could raise to be ambitious, aggressive, open, contemplative, smart, compassionate, curious. The fact that he was a beautiful baby was all right too.

Joshua Collins Stamberg was born in 1970, about the same time that the women's movement began to make an impact. The world was changing. Women, as a group (American, middle-class, mostly white women anyway), refused to be just "beautiful fools." They wanted more. They began having Barnard expectations, were uniting to realize them. What a thrilling time it was! But pendulums have occasional bumps to their swings. I took Josh in his stroller over to a women's meeting I'd read about on a neighborhood lamp-post flyer. When I rolled him into the room, every head turned in horror. They looked at me as if I'd contaminated the place, simply because I was a mother with a child. (They had no idea I'd been a professional broadcaster for some eight years at that point, a career woman *and* a wife and mother. That wouldn't have mattered. It was the sight of that baby carriage that stopped all conversation.)

So growing up female in the seventies was a very different kettle of foolishness. That's what I mean about my generation's having had the toughest experience. We had to straddle simpishness and social reform. We had to take the Good Girls' brains out for an airing, toughen them up, and begin to function as full human beings, with ambitions and entitlements not unlike those of the men we loved and married. The seventies were exhilarating because of all the ways we reinvented ourselves. We had a sense of infinite possibility that came with learning that "the personal is political." And we began to do something about it.

Susan Stamberg

Gloria Feldt

Gloria Feldt joined the Planned Parenthood Federation of America in 1974 and was president of both the Federation and its political arm, the Planned Parenthood Action Fund from 1996 until 2005. She has published two books, The War on Choice: The Right Wing Attack on Women's Rights and How to Fight Back *and* Behind Every Choice Is a Story. *She and her husband, Alex Barbanell, have six children, nine grandchildren, and one great-grandchild.*

THE FAMILY LEGEND has it that when my mother was pregnant with me, my father (always a larger-than-life kind of guy) bragged loudly to everyone that "he" was going to have a boy. When I turned out to be a girl, he immediately started bragging loudly about his daughter. My grandmother reminded him, "Max, you bragged that you were having a boy." To which he bellowed, "Who said I wanted a boy?!"

Now, you might have noticed that my mother's voice wasn't represented in that story. This was not unusual. My parents were yin and yang—they had complementary neuroses. Daddy was totally active. Mother was totally passive. And Grandmother turned out to be my closest childhood companion and role model, but I'll get to that later.

The active and passive competed for my soul throughout my childhood and well into mid-adulthood. Even today, long after I managed to create a pretty good synthesis of what I consider the better parts of their respective personalities, I still sometimes catch myself whipsawing between bowling people over and standing back mute.

When I was three, Daddy bought me a magnificent electric train. A big one with lots of moving parts. It made these great sparks and hissing noises as it traveled around the track. He always treated me like a mini adult. At his initiation, I often went along with him and my mother on business trips. He took me flying in his Beechcraft Bonanza every Sunday. He told me, "You can do anything your pretty little head desires."

My mother's insecurities and passivity tipped the scale and generally held sway in my psyche all through my childhood years, which I spent in small-town Texas during the 1940s and 1950s. I could be willful, but not very strong-willed. In a culture that did not encourage girls to aspire to anything other than becoming a wife and mother, I hid my intelligence and aspirations under a bushel basket. I was a bookish kid; my favorite summer pastime was curling up in Grandmother's big burgundy easy chair and reading one of the twelve books a week I checked out of the library, having utilized the collective library cards of both grandmothers, my mother, and myself to the hilt. I made mostly straight A's, except for art and algebra—but then girls weren't expected to do well in math (except by my father, for whom there seemed to be only two grades: If it wasn't an A, it might as well have been an F).

More than anything, I yearned to be "normal," like everyone else. Being from the only Jewish family in town exacerbated this typical teenage goal. When the adolescent hormones kicked in, I became a teenage jelly woman, molding my behavior and my body to be what I thought society, and especially teenage boys, wanted me to be. At fifteen, I became pregnant and got married—in that order—and set forth quite deliberately to be what I perceived to be the all-American woman—cooking, cleaning, packing my husband's lunch, and having babies. Nobody talked to me or my friends about having sex or birth control. Little did I know just how "normal" I was, for that year, 1957, marked the highest teen-pregnancy rate our country has ever seen. This surprises most people when I tell them, but it's true, and the average age of marriage was eighteen.

Those were the days when women couldn't get credit without a male cosponsor, when help-wanted ads were divided into clearly defined male and female columns. When there was no Title IX and no female admission to many colleges. Birth control was illegal in some states and inaccessible in most; it was still largely limited to diaphragms and condoms. Abortion was illegal, but we all knew stories of women who had unsafe abortions and who died, almost died, or became infertile as a result.

At twenty, with three children, I was exhausted, and as much as I loved them, I knew another one would do me in.

The birth control pill came out at that time, and it saved my life. Somewhere in the back of my mind, Daddy was always saying, "You can do anything your pretty little head desires." By her example, my grandmother—who had earned a college degree against her family's wishes and worked as a schoolmistress in Bolshevik Russia after the revolution—told me to get an education, that life could be pretty exciting if you broke the mold. It seemed like a lightbulb went off in my head, and I began to see new possibilities for my life—a purpose for the intelligence I'd hidden. I started college and got involved in social-justice work, first as a volunteer, then part-time work, then full-time. My strength of character blossomed like a rose whose petals unfurl a bit at a time as it matures.

I still battle with that old feeling of passivity from time to time. Gradually my father's active voice has taken precedence. The courage to act, I found, requires practice. The fastest route to self-esteem is to stand up for what you believe.

Patti LaBelle

Patti LaBelle has had six gold- or platinum-selling disks released over a twenty-year span and has won two Grammys. She was the recipient of the Soul Train Lifetime Achievement Award in 1997 and also received an honorary doctorate from Boston's prestigious Berklee College of Music. Besides her musical career, she has worked in movies, in television, and on the stage. She has appeared on Broadway, been nominated for three Emmys, and picked up a CableACE Award for her performance with sister soul divas Dionne Warwick and Gladys Knight in Sisters in the Name of Love. *Her autobiography is titled* Don't Block the Blessings.

ONE SIGNIFICANT THING I remember about growing up female is being molested. I remember being a young girl who was open to men, older men. I was a vulnerable, innocent female child, and I was molested by an older man. Thank God he never penetrated me, but he used to fondle me, and the memories still come back every now and then. I remember everything about him—his name, what he looked like. I was thirteen years old.

The one thing that I can say to other women is that you shouldn't blame yourself—you didn't make it happen. A lot of victims of molestation are innocent girls like I was, so it's not about what you're portraying to the predators out there. It's not you, it's them.

*Patti
La Belle*

Carol Moseley Braun

Carol Moseley Braun was born in Chicago on August 16, 1947. She is a graduate of the Chicago public schools and received her bachelor of arts degree from the University of Illinois in 1969 and her law degree in 1972 from the University of Chicago. In 1992, she won election to the United States Senate and achieved a number of firsts: first female senator from Illinois, first female African-American senator, first African-American Democratic senator. After leaving the Senate, she was appointed U.S. ambassador (1999–2001) to New Zealand.

I SPENT MY SUMMERS as a child on a farm in Alabama, which is one of the reasons I think of myself as a farm girl, even today. Everybody laughs at that, but in my own vision of myself, I am a farm girl. My great grandfather purchased the farm in 1870 during that little window of opportunity for blacks after the Civil War. It is still in the family. I have great affection and a sense of connectedness to it.

My great grandmother, with whom I spent those summers, was one of those women who had to run the farm after her husband died. She had people who worked on the farm, and it was productive back then. She wore long skirts and kept a gun in her apron pocket—she was a woman of her own time. I followed behind her as she collected rents and attended to her business. She was fearless and competent and a role model for me.

The farm experience for me was very liberating. It was an environment in which women were equal in every way. Black women have never had the luxury of being able to rely on men to take care of them. Slave families were too often split up, and even after the Civil War, our men were too often unable to take care of their families. We have always had to be prepared to take care of ourselves. If we were "lucky enough" to marry well, we might not have to make a living on our own, but that was the rare situation. In any event, a woman who married well too often gave up her independence and ability to function in the "outside world." One of my aunts was married to a Reverend and never ventured into the world of work, but when he died, this woman was a fish out of water with no clue how to manage. I did *not* want to be like her.

To grow up female is to be inventive. Girls have to invent ways to express their personhood, their spirit, around and through and in spite of societal assumptions, preconditions, and strictures that consign women to a particular set of roles. While on the one hand those roles might be fine, they are also by definition limited and defined by power arrangements that depend on gender.

Whether a woman wants to do something outside or even within the roles that have been assigned to her, she has to be inventive. Women who stay in the home and take on the traditional roles of being helpmates and supporters to their husbands have to be inventive in getting things to go their way. Sometimes they have to be clever enough to make him think it was his idea. Sometimes they need to manipulate and work through barriers and jump hurdles to do what they think is in their own best interest. Those who decide to work outside the home and work in the world have to be inventive in reconciling their interests and their vision with what it is that they're expected to do or, conversely, not to do. Our feminine challenge lies in keeping the lessons of the past in front of us as we move toward an unknown and undefined future.

When I was small, I was very taken with the glamour of the adventurers and the explorers of the African and South American jungles. I told my mother that I wanted to be an adventurer and stow away on a tramp steamer. I didn't have any idea of what a tramp steamer was, but I was going to stow away on one and see the world. Her response was, "Girls don't do things like that." I was very annoyed and unable to understand. "Well, *why* don't girls do things like that? Girls can't see the world? Girls can't get around and do interesting things with their lives?" She was careful to explain to me that I could still do things that I wanted to do, but that there were just different ways that girls had to do them. I've been frustrated by that conversation for more than fifty years.

The contradictory message that we give girls—and that my mother gave me—is that you can be what you want to be, but not overtly. You can contribute to the society, but only in "appropriate" ways. You can exercise your intellect, but don't make the boys think you are too smart. My family prized intellectual achievement and developing one's mind and one's talents. They promoted those values while at the same telling me, "You can learn rhetoric but you can't give a speech in public. You might know the answer, but you should not raise your hand in class." The contradictions between the status assigned to women and the expressed values of intellectual freedom frustrated and confounded me. Those contradictions required all of us to figure out ways to be our authentic selves in spite of the limitations.

From the beginning, I refused to step back. The ups and the downs of my life have been defined by my inability to see those limitations or even to be able to see how other people perceive those limitations. This "blind spot" has been both a benefit and a curse. There have been times when I have been a pioneer because it was the right thing to do at that time, without regard for the opinions of others or the traditional limitations of my gender.

When I got to the Senate, for example, I went to work one day wearing a very nice pantsuit. I walked onto the Senate floor, not thinking twice about it, and nobody said anything to me about it. The next day, an article in the local paper stated that I was the first woman in history to wear pants on the Senate floor. This caused a great commotion, as the women employees in the Senate then insisted on their right to wear pants to work. After all, if a Senator could wear pants, why couldn't they? It was Pantsuit Lib! I suppose the story would be different if I set out deliberately to violate the pants rule. I didn't. I just wore what I thought was sensible clothing to work.

Women approach power differently from the way men do. I think it's an offshoot of having to be inventive. We tend to seek win-win solutions, ones that will appeal to everybody. So, our approach to problem solving is different. We go into negotiations not looking to destroy the opposition but rather to co-opt it, and to collaborate with it if necessary. If you can't co-opt or collaborate, *then* you destroy. The point is that the approach is different in feminine uses of power. That's not to say that the outcomes are not the same, because very often they are. I haven't found a huge difference between the kinds of policy positions taken by conservative women and those taken by conservative men. What binds them is their conservativism, and gender does not overcome that. However, conservative women will *approach* the issues differently than conservative men will. I think that that begins to define some of the distinctions between feminine and masculine uses of power.

Be inventive, be yourself, and understand that the fences that limit women deprive the world of half of the talent, the capacity, the genius that might otherwise be available to it. Women should be no more afraid of exercising power in public affairs than they are in their private worlds. You must learn to be your authentic self and understand that you fence yourself in as much as others ever could when you buy into any notion that there are gender-imposed limitations on your choices. You're better off just trying to do something without regard to those limitations and occasionally getting slapped down than telling yourself no and not even trying.

Don't be the one to tell yourself no. You owe it to the world, women and men alike, to reach for the best that you can be, contribute the most you can give, and live your life without reservation.

Carol Moseley Braun

Anne Glauber

Anne Glauber, executive vice president and director of Global Issues Communications for Ruder Finn, is the founder of the Business Council for Peace and serves on the executive council of that organization. Her articles written on behalf of clients have appeared in major newspapers, including the Wall Street Journal, the New York Times, the Washington Post, the Financial Times, and the International Herald Tribune.

DINNERTIME SET THE TONE of my family. Exactly at 5:00 P.M., not a minute later, no matter what we were doing, we had to have dinner. Dad had come home from work. He would be with us for half an hour, before he rushed back to work again. All activity had to stop so we could eat with him; yet he did not speak much to the family during that half hour. His mind was on his business, a difficult one that he loved and had built to be highly successful. So my mother, my brother, and I would chatter among ourselves, making sure not to annoy my father with too much loud talking or laughter.

I grew up in a small town in northeastern Pennsylvania, where traditional roles for women were the norm. Although my mother is a strong, determined, action-oriented woman, the cues growing up were those of the importance of men. She made sure that my father was the center when he did arrive home. Child rearing he left to my mother, who managed the home and paid close, loving attention to the details of our lives. She served my father and catered to his needs. So although Dad was absent from home during most of our waking hours, the significance of men and male authority was very much present.

We were fortunate to have the involvement of our grandparents in our lives. We were all devoted to my mother's father, Bobby, who captured the grandchildren's attention and love through his unusual way of looking at life, utterly optimistic and full of appreciation for its absurdities. He would dispense his wisdom through the songs he taught us and the Jewish proverbs he made us memorize. He taught us about loving nature and finding joy in the small details of life. My brother and I adored him. He was king. He had three daughters who doted on him, and his sweet, loving wife, my grandmother, who served his every need and whim. She put herself last and listened to whatever he told her to do.

Somehow in the midst of this, I rebelled in secret. The sense of women serving men seemed so unfair. I worked hard to avoid the female duties of the household, purposely not cleaning my room or finding excuses not to do the dishes alongside my mom, wondering why my younger brother evaded the jobs more easily.

I read stories of Eleanor Roosevelt and claimed her as my hero. I immersed myself in books about historical

figures, men and women, who by the force of their character overcame significant external and internal obstacles to
achieve success and contribute to the betterment of society.
Looking back, I understand that I equated being a girl with
seeing obstacles in my path that somehow demanded some
internal strength to overcome.

So I gravitated to women in my small town who seemed
different from the norm, who seemed to be living a different
pattern: the widow who had a sarcastic wit, a reckless laugh,
and a live-in lover; the rabbi's wife, who in her physical
stature and massive personality dominated her small, shy
husband. And then, of course, there was my father's mother,
my other grandmother.

At the age of eight, I learned that she was really not my
father's mother. She was his aunt. The story always captivated
me. My grandmother, Rose, had been living an independent
life, working at her career in the Pentagon. In 1936, her sister,
my father's natural mother, died of pneumonia, leaving two
small children under the age of six and a husband devastated
by the loss. Her family called her home. She was the unmarried sister in a large family of nine siblings. Her parents told
her to marry my grandfather and become a mother to his
children. She did not love him. She did her duty.

The headline from the yellowed wedding announcement
is about her brother: "Reuben Levy's sister marries." She is
invisible. I think about the sacrifice, her denying her own
ambitions to raise her nephews and support my grandfather.
She put her energies and strong intelligence into the business that my grandfather started and where my father as-

sumed the leadership in his adult life. She worked daily with my grandfather, managing the finances and planning business strategies, demonstrating how her acumen could take a small storefront and build it into a major enterprise.

She raised the boys and managed her home with elegance and taste, always dressed with sophistication and flair, and became a model of a woman who could balance many aspects of a varied life and do it well. She never talked about any of the sacrifices, but by watching her I felt that women were capable of an unnameable strength and resilience, which enabled us, even when we forgot it was there, to prevail.

My mother helped me do that as well. We were one of the few Jewish families in a small Pennsylvanian coal-mining town. Growing up a true minority made my brother and me very proud of our Jewish identity and culture. One day, in sixth grade, I had a major fight with three girls in my neighborhood. It is difficult now to recall the particulars: We were walking the six blocks to school; it was close to Easter; someone asked me if I thought Jesus was God, and I defiantly said, "No." With that, the girls started walking faster and left me on the pavement to walk to school on my own. They stopped talking to me, and after several days I was miserable. At the same time, we were doing plays in science class about germs and cells. The girls in my neighborhood were to be in my play, which I had written and in which I had given everyone major parts—the germ, the cell, the body, the vaccine. One of the girls wrote me a note to say that they would not be in the play and in fact were doing their own.

The play was two days away. I ran home crying and told my mother about the predicament.

She did not hesitate for a moment. "You play all the parts," she said. I looked at her with astonishment and wondered how that could be possible. But she helped me make it work. I changed costumes, changed voices, and for the germ I had a fake mustache to represent the evil invasion. I even had him die a horrible death in the throes of penicillin shock. The play was a rousing success. The teacher and the students gave me a standing ovation. And I received the ultimate honor, performing the play, on my own again, for the entire school at assembly. The girls started talking to me the next day.

The theme in all the biographies I was reading of strong people overcoming obstacles was taught to me that day, plainly and simply, by my mother. We can defy external perceptions of our capabilities and marshal our own creativity and inner strength to achieve what we define as success. And needless to say, I have taken my mother's counsel to heart!

Like countless women, I continue to "play all the parts"—single mother, public-relations executive, businesswoman, social activist.

Anne Friedman Glauber

Jamie-Lynn Sigler

Long Island native Jamie-Lynn Sigler began singing and acting at the age of seven. Best known for her role as Meadow Soprano in HBO's The Sopranos, *she made her Broadway debut in 2002 as Belle in Disney's* Beauty and the Beast, *and that same year Pocket Books published her autobiography,* Wise Girl: What I've Learned about Life, Love, and Loss.

THE WORD THAT SUMS UP growing up female to me is "rewarding." We face many obstacles in our lives—relationships, careers, motherhood—and though they all may be difficult and challenging, they are all incredibly rewarding. We put hard work, emotions, love, and tears into these experiences, and they give us their own individual satisfactions. As females, we take on many roles, in the workplace and in our families, and we have the ability to make a difference. When we do, it is incredibly rewarding.

Growing up, the most important thing in my world was my mother. Always and forever. She has endured an incredible amount of hardship in her life. She taught me about appreciation and love and that in the end family and health are everything. Without my mom, I don't think that I would ever have the perceptions that I have today. Though it hurts to know that my mom had to go through so many rough times, I am so proud of the woman that she has become. I only hope that I can be half the mom she is. God willing, one day.

When I was really young, all I wanted to do was hang out with my two older brothers. They were the epitome of cool, and I would have done anything just to be allowed into their circle. And so my life from the age of two through five was all about sports. While I loved my dresses and Barbies, I needed to rough it in the dirt and mud to be with them. And I had fun! I loved baseball and hockey. I have incredible memories of cheering them on at their Little League games.

When I started ballet class at five, things changed. I truly believed at one point that my calling was to be a ballerina. I loved being onstage. I loved the grace and beauty of dance. I loved the costumes! For years, I would get picked up from ballet class and change in the back of the car into my soccer/tennis/softball attire until I was finally able to let go and realize that it was OK to be different from my brothers. And of course they loved me just as much, and maybe even more, for my individuality. It meant a lot when all of a sudden they were coming to cheer me on at my dance recitals! I am incredibly close to my brothers, and the three of us couldn't be more different. We support and love each other for who we are, as individuals.

Growing up female is not easy. It is difficult, confusing,

and frustrating, but at the same time incredibly wonderful. We all, at different times, get to a certain amazing place in our lives where we embrace who we are both physically and emotionally. I believe that all females find this at some point in their lives, and when they do, it finally becomes clear how amazing it is to be a woman.

♡ Jamie-Lynn Sigler

Regina King

Born and brought up in Los Angeles, Regina King first came to public attention in the television sitcom 227, *which ran for five seasons, during which time she graduated from Westchester High School. After her TV series ended, she worked in John Singleton's* Boyz N the Hood *and the cult comedy* Friday, *then moved on to her much-praised role as Cuba Gooding's wife in* Jerry Maguire. *Since that time, she has appeared in many more films, including* Daddy Day Care, Legally Blonde 2: Red, White & Blonde *and the Oscar award–winning* Ray

THERE IS A POINT in your life when you *think* you are a woman and your mother *knows* you are not. I suspect that for most women, this point arrives between the ages of fifteen and eighteen. This happened to me when I was almost seventeen.

During that time, I remember wanting to get a tattoo. My mother said, "There is no need to mark up beautiful skin, and that won't be happening under my roof." I also wanted to move in with my boyfriend. She said, "You need to have a plan and know yourself before you bring someone else into the equation."

Soon after my seventeenth birthday, I did exactly what my mother had told me not to. I moved in with my boyfriend and got a tattoo on my shoulder so that everyone could see it when I wore a tank top. I lived with my boyfriend for only three months (I'll leave out the details of his departure), and the tattoo still bothers me to this day. I spend extra time in the makeup chair to cover it up when I'm shooting a project. I have never had a role that called for a tattoo, and though I thought that I had chosen a unique symbol, many others today share the same tattoo.

These two memories, among others, continue to remind me of how far from being a woman I really was back then. These two situations have also helped me keep from merely hearing, and I have started actually listening. I am also constantly reminded of my mother's favorite words, the seven *P*'s: Proper prior preparation prevents piss-poor performance.

Esther Hautzig

Hautzig's 1969 classic, The Endless Steppe, *an autobiographical account of her life from ages ten to fifteen, was a National Book Award finalist and an American Library Association Notable Book of the Year. She has published a variety of work, from craft books for children to books involving her Jewish heritage, such as* A Gift for Mama, Remember Who You Are: Stories About Being Jewish, Riches, *and* A Picture of Grandmother, *which was named a 2002 Sydney Taylor Honor Book for Older Readers by the Association of Jewish Libraries. She has translated two volumes of stories from Yiddish,* The Case Against the Wind *and* Seven Good Years. *Her interest in getting children involved in learning other languages has resulted in a Four Languages series of books, containing text in English, Spanish, French, and Russian.*

I WAS BORN IN 1930, in Vilna, also known as Wilno when it was part of Poland and Vilnius when it was and is now the capital of Lithuania.

In June 1941, my parents, paternal grandparents, and I were arrested by the Soviet government and deported to Siberia as capitalists and enemies of the people. This probably saved us

BECOMING MYSELF

from death in the Vilna ghetto or in a Nazi concentration camp. Papa's father was separated from us and sent to the gulag, where he later died. We and Grandmother were loaded onto a truck and then transferred to cattle cars at the Vilna railroad station. After six weeks, we arrived in Rubtsovsk, a tiny village on the Siberian steppe.

All the deportees were lined up in the village square, to be chosen for work in the area. Our family was ordered to work in a gypsum mine, hours away from the village.

Mama was to drill holes in which dynamite would be placed and exploded to enlarge the mines. Papa was to harness a horse to a cart, which would then be filled with gypsum and transported elsewhere on the steppe.

Papa found cause for laughter wherever he was. He would harness the poor animal, get into the cart, click his tongue, and the horse would trot off, Papa holding the reins and laughing. That made life bearable.

After many weeks of being crowded into the one-room schoolhouse on the steppe and sleeping on straw pallets on the floor, we received an amnesty from the Soviet government that was negotiated with the Polish government in exile. No more sleeping with twenty-six other deportees!

After that, we were permitted to return to the village, where housing would hopefully be found. We were assigned to live with another family from Vilna and a young couple with a new baby, all in one small room. Two wooden platforms served as our beds (though we had no mattresses), and we had a table with a few benches, a stove, and some shelves.

There was a lean-to against this hut where wood and coal was stored, and an outhouse nearby.

The young couple had a bed near one window, and the baby's crib was suspended from the ceiling. They were plain and kind people, who could not believe that we were Jews. Jews had long beards, black hair, and big noses!

Growing up female in Siberia was not much different from growing up—period. Everyone in the village was assigned to work, the children went to school six days a week, and on many Sundays we were expected to volunteer to help the war effort.

FOR SOME REASON, I was to be the family's emissary to the *barakholka,* a kind of flea market, with open stalls, tables, or barrels, selling sunflower seeds, sometimes bread and flour, oil or sugar.

My mission was to sell or barter things, which Mama hurriedly packed in a very brief span of time. Some of her choices were not too useful in Siberia. Grandmother came with me at times, but more often I went by myself.

At first, I was somewhat befuddled by it all, but I adjusted as my knowledge of Russian improved. Sometimes I made a sale, other times I bartered for something to eat. Food was very scarce by then. Ration cards were distributed to all the inhabitants of Rubtsovsk, but the natives had an edge on those who did not have land on which to plant a garden.

Sometimes I roamed in the fields outside the village,

where natives had been assigned plots of land where they could plant potatoes. A little four-year-old boy would tag along with me and we would dig for potatoes the natives left in the ground; most of them were either rotted or frozen. Still we took them back to our lodgings.

I knitted for a woman with one arm who wanted a scarf and sweater for her little girl, and I got paid with vegetables from her garden.

Over the years in Siberia, I learned to whitewash walls, to stomp with bare feet inside an enclosure where cow manure, straw, and clay were mixed and then loaded into wooden frames to dry out and harden and then be used for building huts on the Siberian steppe. I collected onion peelings and boiled them to make a yellow dye to transform hospital gauze into curtains for one of the huts where we lived.

Mama was not an effusive person; she seldom praised me with words. Early on, I could tell by her face and eyes when she was pleased with something I had done.

As an only child, even in Vilna, I sometimes spoke to myself. Whenever she overheard me, Mama said, very quietly, "You are speaking to a very smart person," or "You are in very good company, my child."

Once she mentioned that another deportee from Vilna had commented that I walked in the village as if I were the daughter of one of the *nachalniks* (big shots) in the factory from Kharkov. I wasn't sure it was a compliment until Mama added, "Hold your head high and do the best you can."

The time came when I could no longer squeeze my feet into the shoes I wore when we left Vilna. I had signed up for a declamation contest and memorized "Tatyana's Dream" from Pushkin's poem *Eugene Onegin.* The contest was to take place during the summer at the school I attended. When I arrived, sweaty and scared, the teacher looked me in the eye and refused to let me go onstage, because I was barefoot.

I ran back to our hut, grabbed Grandmother's slippers and some string, and raced back to school. With the slippers tied with string on my feet, I was the last contestant to participate. Needless to say, I lost.

What was I to do? I overheard grown-ups talking about a deportee who got a shipment from the Red Cross in Switzerland. Maybe he got shoes? I took a piece of newspaper, put down my foot, and drew the outline to indicate the size of shoes that might fit me. I went all by myself to the hut where the man lived. He was rude and harsh. I can still see his face when I go out now to buy new shoes. He had no idea of the strength of my determination once I'd made up my mind to succeed.

After many more humiliating trips to his hut, I did get a pair of new shoes, which I wiped with the hem of my dress or skirt each time I wore them on the dusty steppe.

One day when I was trading almost the last tradable goods in our possession on the *barakholka,* a kindly man stopped to examine my wares. He seemed more interested in talking with me than in considering the goods I held in my hands. For a reason I cannot decipher to this day, I said to this sweet and gentle man, "I think you will like my family. Please come to visit us."

Perhaps it was a subconscious recollection of Elijah, who

stopped to talk with the poor porter Tovye in I. L. Peretz's story "The Seven Good Years." The man came to visit, but he was not Elijah—he was Yosif Yudovich Ostrow. His wife, whose nickname was Zaya, was beautiful and as kind as her husband. Henceforth they became our guardian angels, and my beloved Uncle Yozia and Aunt Zaya. They saved us after Papa was drafted.

I was sick in bed with a high fever. Having Papa go off to war yet another time was more than I could handle. In 1939, when he was drafted into the Polish army and was declared dead, Mama said he'd come back. "Don't worry, he *will* come back." And he did. This time was different. We were not in Vilna with family all around us. Mama looked as if she would cry—which scared me more than anything. Mama did not cry. Mama was always calm. Mama could handle anything. She said she would go to see Uncle Yozia and Aunt Zaya. "They will help us." Mama never asked for help. But help came.

Uncle Yozia had a friend in the factory where they worked. His friend's wife and children had to go to care for her ill parents, and he would need someone to help him in his home.

Our duties—and I truly mean *our* duties—were to clean the house, wash his laundry, iron shirts, and make sure that there was a meal waiting for him when he returned from work. Since he was one of the managers of the tractor factory, he came home late on most evenings. More often than not, he wobbled a bit and seemed inebriated.

Uncle Yozia's friend was very respectful of Mama and kind to me. The best part of our move was that I could transfer to the school adjacent to the tractor factory and to the new and special housing for the management.

The teachers in that school were professors of literature in universities, teachers of science, algebra, geometry, history, geography (according to the Communist dogma), and foreign languages. They were evacuated from Europe: Moscow, Leningrad, and other major cities. The professor of Russian literature in Moscow had to deal with students not on her level of expertise. Her name was Anna Semyonovna, and she seemed interested in my comments. The highlight of my education in Siberia was being asked by Anna Semyonovna to read my essay on Pushkin's short story "The Captain's Daughter" to the entire class. No subsequent honor has ever meant so much to me. I still see her face, with gray hair parted in the middle and collected in a bun on the back of her head. I remember her intelligent eyes and attentiveness to my presentation.

Teachers of subjects in mathematics and science wrung their hands and shook their heads at my inability to remember a single equation, add up numbers correctly, prepare some semblance of understanding in homework I dutifully turned in. Geometry was the only subject in that field that I could pass, but only barely.

The time with Uncle Yozia's friend reached an end and we had to find new housing. He came to our aid again and helped us find a tiny room in the home of a local couple. I had to sleep on a box the size of a hope chest, squeezed between a wall and a Siberian version of an armoire in which we kept all our belongings.

If I wanted to stretch out, I had to put my legs up, vertically. To this day, however, I sleep curled up, with my knees practically by my chin.

I do believe that being a girl at that time and in that place was a huge advantage for me. I had life skills—cooking, knitting, cleaning, bartering, sewing, turning shirt collars on shirts that had seen better days, painting walls, planting a garden—the last of these my grandfather had taught us in Vilna. He assigned a little space to each grandchild in his flower beds, in which we were to plant vegetables. When people questioned this anomaly, he would smile and say, "You never know when a person will need food!" He was likely to inspect everyone's crop to see if it was well tended, weeded, watered. Those of us who met his standards were praised, blessed, and given a big kiss and hug.

All these skills were lifesavers in Rubtsovsk.

I learned never to give up in Siberia, or anywhere else for that matter. Mama's remark that I walked like the child of a *nachalnik* remained with me in Siberia and does to this day. Now when I take on projects that seem overwhelming, I remember that advice, and it empowers me.

Esther Rudomin Hautzig

Kate Spade

Katherine Noel Brosnahan grew up in Kansas City, Missouri, and attended college at Arizona State University, where she majored in broadcast journalism. In 1991, after five years in the fashion department at Mademoiselle *magazine, she decided to start her own business. Combining her name with then boyfriend, now husband, Andy Spade, Kate started a handbag business.*

Kate has received a number of important awards from the fashion industry, including the Council of Fashion Designers of America Perry Ellis Award for New Fashion Talent. In 1999, the Spades sold 56 percent of their internationally successful business to Neiman Marcus for $33.6 million.

KANSAS CITY WAS A GREAT PLACE to grow up. I really loved hopping onto my bike and riding around town until dusk. You'd hear your name being called to come in for dinner. There was a sense of security and peace back then. Now you always have to watch your back—don't do this, don't do that.

I was born fifth out of six children in my family. Number four of five girls. A real posse. My parents were divorced, and we lived with my mother, so it was a very female household, a lot of fun with all the sisters. I had this great perspective of being able to look at things through my sisters' eyes as they grew older. I was always anticipating getting to where they were. The same was true of my mother. I would look at the things she did and think, *I can't wait till I can do that.*

It was hard to wait for my own room. My oldest sister and my brother always had their own rooms. When my sister moved out, the next-oldest got the room. She had a little brass door knocker with her name on it. I would walk in and watch her do her homework by herself with her radio on and think, *Oh, I cannot wait.* A room of one's own.

I also remember thinking about how great it would be to get my own job, to get a paycheck and be responsible for myself. My sister Ann had a job as a hostess in a restaurant. She thought her long dress with ruffles was the ugliest thing in the world. If I were to look at it now, I'm sure it was, but back then I thought how pretty it was and how much I loved that dress.

We would play like we had jobs. My sister had a vanity in her bedroom that always ended up being the desk where the boss sat, and I was always the secretary. I couldn't wait to be the one who sat in the boss's chair—I thought that meant you worked less and were able to do whatever you wanted. When my turn finally came, my little sister, Eve, became the underling. I didn't even give her a name. It was how I perceived what a boss would be like. I'd say, "Secretary, I'd like a cup of coffee. Secretary, I need more pens. Secretary, where are my messages?"

I did a lot of babysitting when I was eleven or twelve.

In the afternoons, I took care of all the babies in the neighborhood so their mothers could run errands. They were very secure, because my mother was next door. One summer, my very best friend, Susie, and I decided to have a little school. We had eight, maybe ten kids in our backyard, and three days a week we took them to the park for two hours. We supplied the Kool-Aid and the entertainment, and they had to bring their own lunch. Having the money we made was a big deal for me. My mother said, "Don't tell everyone in the family about how much money you have, because they're going to want to borrow it." That night at dinner, it was the first thing out of my mouth. "I made twenty-five dollars!" My mom says, when she tells the story these days, "Sure enough, I could see your older sister, Ann, coming into your room, followed by your brother."

The money was my money. My parents were very good about letting me spend it, unless it was on something horrible that they wouldn't let me buy. I remember thinking, *I can buy what I want.* If it was a shirt that Mom didn't like, I could pay for it. As I got a little older, shopping for clothes meant going to vintage stores. When I was fourteen, I read an article in *Seventeen* about how you could find great things at the Salvation Army. My mother would drive me down to the Salvation Army and another store called Past Time. I would buy things like a leopard coat and chartreuse green short gloves. I think my mom got a little thrill out of my purchases, because these were things she might have worn in the 1960s. But I never imagined that I was going to be a designer.

My friend Susie and I had become best friends in the second grade. And to this day, we're still just thick as thieves. We're really the best friends in the whole wide world. We talk all the time. We know everything about one another. As kids, we were very loyal. That was at an age when girls say things about each other, but no one would have dared say anything to me about Susie, or vice versa. We supported each other. We had great imaginations, and we did a lot of very funny things.

When we were about eleven, we boarded a bus and rode to Union Station to get on a train. Our parents thought we were down the street in the park. We'd sit on the train and think, *Wouldn't it be great if the train started to move?* Our parents wouldn't have thought it was so funny if they had to come to St. Louis to pick us up, but we thought it was great.

There was a church down the street, and Susie and I would go in and pretend we were giving a sermon when no one was there. One day, someone in the church said we'd have to leave, because there was going to be a wedding. Susie and I looked at each other. "Oh, really?" We went home and got dressed up, and we went to the wedding. I ran into someone who knew my mother, and I said, "Oh, we don't have a ride. May we have a ride to the reception?" We got a ride to the reception and afterward had to take a taxi home. I would never have done this sort of thing by myself, but when it was with my dearest friend, we just said, "Oh, let's try it."

My mom was my role model. She was from the "mind your manners" and "always obey" school. We tease her now, but we would never have dared to back then. I give her a lot of credit. She was a single parent with six children, and she allowed and encouraged us to carve out our own identity. Encouraged us to cultivate our own sense of who we were. This instilled a lot of confidence in me.

Another influence on me was *The Mary Tyler Moore Show.* Mary had her own apartment, she had a job, she had a car and a boss. She had a best friend, Rhoda. She and Rhoda were completely different in the way Susie and I were different. They curled their hair together and ate popcorn at night and cried to one another. I would imagine myself in this great apartment in New York. It was all about independence. It's funny, because that's what I thought I'd end up doing—working at a news station. I met Mary Tyler Moore once, and I told her how inspirational that show was to me. I'm sure she's heard it a thousand times.

Once I did get out on my own, I never I felt that I couldn't do something because I was a female. I was growing up in the era of Gloria Steinem and the ERA. There's an area in Kansas City called the Plaza, and there was a big protest rally where they were trying to sign women up. I wasn't old enough to sign up, but I asked what the ERA was. They explained it to me, and I thought, *Yeah, of course, isn't that the way it already is?* That's probably the first time I realized that it wasn't the way it was. Even when I entered the workforce, it didn't seem to be a problem. I worked at Condé Nast with all women. My day-to-day contacts were with the editor in chief, the fashion director, the beauty director, the articles director, and they were all women.

I wish girls would worry less. It's a waste of time to worry so much, and that includes both about how you look and what you do. I'm not saying to be arrogant, but just to believe in what you're doing and not be nervous and worried. Find a place of inner security within yourself and say, "Yeah, that's okay."

Lisa Bernhard

Lisa Bernhard joined the Fox News Channel in 2003 as an entertainment correspondent. She reports within the entertainment industry on film, music, television, and celebrity news. Before joining Fox, she was deputy editor of TV Guide, *where she covered major entertainment stories, conducted celebrity interviews, and made numerous appearances on the* Today *show,* The View, *and* Access Hollywood, *among others.*

MY FIRST MEMORY of loving baseball dates back to age seven. That beautiful expanse of green. The cunning duel between pitcher and batter. The languid pace, the surge of excitement. The ball landing—*swish!*—into the web of a mitt and cracking off the end of the bat. The game meant summertime, warmth, purity, simplicity, and joy.

The New York Mets were my favorite team. I'd sit in front of the TV rooting for each player by first *and* last name. I was superstitious that way. I couldn't just say, "C'mon, Tom." I wasn't sure that the baseball god I was praying to knew I meant Tom Seaver, the Mets' ace pitcher. There were lots of Toms playing baseball, after all. I had to be clear, I thought, if I really wanted my team to win.

By the time I was ten, baseball was a huge part of my life. I owned my second mitt by then. I had all the accessories to make me a better player, including a Johnny Bench Batter-Up and a Pitch-Back. There were no Little League teams for girls in my town, but I was fortunate to live among spacious lawns that served as beautiful baseball diamonds.

When I was twelve, I went off to summer camp. I couldn't watch my beloved Mets there—I was too far north. But I knew I could watch the jewel in the crown—the Major League All-Star Game. Nationally telecast, it would be beamed to every remote corner of the country. It was baseball's big event—all the hometown heroes gathered for one great game.

But there was only one way for me to watch: I had to get into the Big House. The Big House was not a place in which they locked you up when you were bad—it was the rambling manse that contained our dining hall, a "telephone room" in which you could occasionally call home, and a cozy den with a television. I had gotten word from a younger boy that his entire bunk was being let into the Big House to watch the game. If younger kids were being let in, surely my spot in the den was secure. I approached the head of the camp.

"Mr. Golden, may I come into the Big House tonight to watch the All-Star Game?"

"*You* want to watch the game?! I don't think so."

"Um, what?" I replied meekly.

"Lisa," Mr. Golden answered, "you just want to be with the boys. You don't like baseball."

I was shocked. Baseball was the love of my life, not boys. "Actually, I love baseball. I'm a huge Mets fan, and I love the All-Star Game. I watch it every year."

"I don't believe you, Lisa. I think you just want to be with the boys. I'm not letting you in."

I felt humiliated. I was a shy kid, and it took a lot of courage for me to approach the head of the camp. Boys *younger* than I was were being given the privilege of watching the game, but I was not. I wasn't taken seriously, dismissed as some kind of boy-crazy prepubescent harlot.

I walked back to my bunk, defeated, deflated, angry, sad, and confused. I was not let in because I was a girl. Denied the thing I loved most. It hurt.

That night, I crawled into bed, thinking about what a great time the boys must be having watching the game. Then a flash: I had a tiny transistor radio that my dad had given me, and a single earplug. Maybe I could find the game on the radio. I spun through the stations on the receiver until, finally, success. I listened to the game through the last beautiful out, long after my fellow campers and counselors had drifted off to sleep. Or so I thought.

As it turned out, one of my counselors had lain awake too, picking up on the faint sounds that came through my earpiece. It was well past my bedtime, but she had let me listen. The next day—unbeknownst to me—she approached the head of the camp. She told him about how I listened on my transistor, fixated on every pitch, every swing, every catch.

That afternoon, Mr. Golden came toward me. Uh-oh. Did he want to tell me one more time that I was a liar?

"Lisa, I owe you an apology," he said.

I stood in stunned silence.

"I heard that you stayed up late to listen to the game on your radio. I should have let you in. You were telling the truth, and I didn't believe you. I'm sorry."

I didn't know what to say. I was shocked that he knew, and I was shocked that he apologized. I still wished that I had seen the game, wished that he had believed me.

It took me some time to sort through what had happened. Then my emotions swelled. I loved that counselor. I loved knowing that she had been awake, allowing me to break my bedtime curfew. I loved that she stood up for me in a quiet yet powerful way. I loved that the man who ran our camp now knew that I had told the truth, knew that girls could love baseball as much as boys could. I was filled with pride, and I soon realized why. In my own small way, I had done what my heroes had done—stepped up to the plate and hit one out of the park. I smiled. I loved my great game now more than ever.

Lisa Bernhard

Margaret Hilary Marshall

Margaret H. Marshall, the first female chief justice of the Massachusetts Supreme Judicial Court, was born and raised in South Africa. She first came to this country as a high school exchange student and later returned to attend Harvard University for her master's degree, and Yale University for her law degree. She was appointed a justice of the Court in November 1996, and named chief justice in September 1999. Among her many awards, she was the first recipient of the Harvard College Women's Professional Achievement Award. She recently authored a majority opinion acknowledging the legality of marriage between same-sex couples in the Commonwealth of Massachusetts.

I GREW UP IN A SMALL, isolated village in rural South Africa. My early childhood was one of comfortable stability. Life was routine there. As a young white child, I was free from worry or concern. These early years gave me a sense of inner security, an expectation that, whatever the changes or challenges, I would always have my family to support me.

I grew up during the apartheid era, when the system of white supremacy was ruthlessly enforced. White and black South Africans had no social contact with each other, and I grew up unaware of the cruel realities all around me. For white children in my village, school and church were the focal point of our lives. (Black children had little access to education—our school was for white children only.) For us, life was predictable. My siblings and I all had the same first-grade teacher. We read the same books, played the same games, saw the same families and faces, year in and year out. The climate was warm and easy. Sports—swimming, tennis—those were our recreation. There was no television. School plays, a school choir, and music competitions were our entertainment. It was, in many ways, a circumscribed life.

My parents were kind, empathetic, and reliable. My father often helped people in their times of trouble, and my mother always treated people, including Black South Africans, with respect and dignity. That was rare in South Africa. My parents' values had an enormous influence on me: kindness, thoughtfulness. We may have lived in an isolated community, but my parents were not rigid in their view of the world. I was scarcely aware, however, of any challenges to apartheid. None of my friends, or my parents' friends, challenged our settled worldview.

A sharp change occurred: I went to university in Johannesburg and became deeply involved in antiapartheid activities. This was in the 1960s, a period of harsh repression in South Africa. The African National Congress (ANC), of which Nelson Mandela was a leader, had recently been outlawed. The leaders of the ANC were imprisoned. The Pan-Africanist Congress and other important antiapartheid groups had been banned. People were sent to prison simply because they opposed apartheid. It was an oppressive, nasty time. To voice opposition to what was happening made one visible and vulnerable.

I was catapulted from the measured security of my predictable life into the raw and exposed world of antiapartheid activities. Now I can look back and see the seeds of my later actions in the values of my parents, in my father's kindness and my mother's dignity.

But the real change happened in 1962. I came as a high school exchange student to the United States, to Wilmington, Delaware. I had never before traveled outside South Africa. (I had never even been on an airplane.) Now I was thrust into a new world, a world of very different expectations, especially for young women. In South Africa, few graduates of my all-white, all-girls high school went to college. At my school in Delaware, there was an expectation that every girl would go to college. My year in the United States opened my eyes, opened my mind. While I was there, I had the opportunity to learn about my own country in a new way. I read books about South Africa—such as Alan Paton's *Cry the Beloved Country*—that were outlawed in South Africa by the apartheid government. I read about my country's history, and the history of struggle by the majority of its people. I was exposed to and thrived on new ideas. I also learned about the civil rights movement, which at the time was vibrant in the United States. I listened to Dr. Martin Luther King Jr. I listened to President John F. Kennedy. As a white child growing up in a secure environment in South

Africa, I had asked few questions. I now learned to ask questions and demand answers.

It is hard for Americans to imagine what it is like to live in a totalitarian society like the South Africa of my childhood—where access to information is censored, the open exchange of ideas is suppressed, intellectuals are persecuted, books are banned, movies are forbidden, and the radio is government-controlled. In a vigorous democracy like America, we may take for granted the freedom to think and speak as we wish. My early childhood, the security and happiness of my early years, gave me a firm foundation. But it was the unexpected, the brief taste of freedom in the United States, that set me in a new direction.

Margaret Marshall
(Due to the rules governing the Supreme Judicial Court of Massachusetts, a Justice's signature is not permitted to be publicly printed.)

Lesléa Newman

Born in Brooklyn, New York, Lesléa Newman attended Jericho High School and graduated from the University of Vermont with a B.S. in education. She then attended the Naropa Institute in Boulder, Colorado, where she was Allen Ginsberg's apprentice. She is the author of fifty books, including Heather Has Two Mommies, A Letter to Harvey Milk, Write from the Heart, *and* Out of the Closet and Nothing to Wear. *Her literary awards include poetry fellowships from the Massachusetts Artists Fellowship Foundation and the National Endowment for the Arts, the* Highlights for Children *Fiction Writing Award, the James Baldwin Award for Cultural Achievement, and three Pushcart Prize nominations. Nine of her books have been Lambda Literary Award finalists.*

GROWING UP FEMALE meant growing up in a female body. A body that was different from those that belonged to my brothers. A body that was treated differently as well.

In one of my earliest memories, I am about five years old and I am standing outside Gussie's Candy Store in Brooklyn, New York. I am holding a cigar-shaped pretzel in one hand and a chocolate milk shake in the other. "Look at her," an aunt of mine said, pointing at me. "She doesn't know what to eat first." The laughter that followed was not kind.

My brothers could eat anything they wanted and remain as thin as the aforementioned pretzel. When we got home from school, my older brother devoured Ring Dings and Yodels; my younger brother scarfed down leaning towers of Oreo cookies. I was given skim milk and carrot sticks. At suppertime when I reached for a roll, my mother snapped, "You don't need that," and moved the plate to the other side of the table. As I grew older, my father threw in his two cents: "Do yourself a favor and lose a little weight."

And so the dieting began. Atkins, Weight Watchers, the drinking man's diet, the thinking man's diet . . . By the time I got to college, I could tell you the calorie content of any food imaginable. I filled the margins of my notebooks with columns of numbers. No, I wasn't a math major. I was adding up the number of calories I had eaten that day, the number of calories I had eaten the day before, the number of calories I planned on eating the next day and the day after that and the day after that. Of course, it was impossible to stick to these rigid diets for very long. Periods of denying myself food were followed by periods of bingeing on sugar-filled cakes, cookies, and ice cream. These binges were followed by more restrictive dieting, which was followed by more excessive bingeing, which was followed by more restrictive dieting.

I had several wardrobes during this time of my life. Clothes that fit, which consisted mostly of baggy sweaters and army pants. Clothes I wished would fit, namely two pairs of size-ten jeans that I could zip myself into if I lay flat on my bed, sucked in my stomach, and didn't breathe for the rest of the day. And clothes I dreaded would fit—the tent dresses that didn't hide my expanding shape even though I convinced myself that they made me look slimmer.

After I graduated from college, I moved to New York City, and my eating became even more dangerous and bizarre. One autumn, I worked as a temporary secretary at the United Nations. I had to look professional, which meant I had to fit into my "thin clothes." So I decided to stop eating altogether. Instead I drank a quart of apple cider a day. I kept a thermos on my desk that I took little sips from throughout the morning and afternoon. I'm sure my coworkers thought I had a drinking problem.

What saved me from completely destroying my health and my body was the feminist movement. I began to meet feminists who denounced the "diet industry" as being oppressive to women. I started attending a support group that encouraged women to throw away our scales and calorie counters and just eat according to our physical hunger. And most important of all, I met strong, courageous, stunning women who loved themselves just as they were, even though they did not look anything like the fashion models I saw on the covers of glossy magazines. With the love and support of these women, I began to do very radical things. I shoved my baggy sweaters to the back of my closet and wore a shirt that actually fit. And more than that—I tucked it in. I really thought somebody (me) would die if I did something so outrageous. But no one did.

Surprisingly, once I gave myself permission to eat whatever I wanted, I actually craved healthy foods like fruits and vegetables. I didn't want to eat chocolate at every meal (though I do love chocolate and eat it, in moderation, on a regular basis). When I gave up dieting, I slowly lost the excess weight I had put on because of my bingeing. After about a year, my weight stabilized. It has remained virtually the same for the past two decades.

I thought I was pretty much done with being obsessed with weight and body image, but I realized that wasn't so when a friend of mine went hiking with a female companion who was struck and killed by lightning. The young woman left behind a diary filled with self-loathing entries about her weight and her body. And before I knew it, I had penned a novel entitled *Fat Chance,* which is the fictional diary of a teenage girl who develops an eating disorder. I was amazed at how easily the writing came to me and how acutely I remembered what it was like to hate myself so vehemently. I have received many letters from young girls who tell me that reading *Fat Chance* was like reading the story of their own lives. It makes me tremendously sad to know that growing up female is still so painful to so many when it doesn't have to be.

I have made peace with my female body now that I am older, softer, more wrinkled, and—dare I say it—more beautiful. I know that my body will never be "perfect" by others' standards. But I also know that my body is perfect by the only standard that counts—my own.

Lesléa Newman

Kate Winslet

Born to Roger Winslet and Sally Bridges-Winslet, both English stage actors, Kate Winslet attracted attention over a decade ago as Juliet Hulme in Peter Jackson's Heavenly Creatures *(1994). In 1995, she received the first of two Academy Award nominations as Best Supporting Actress for her role in Ang Lee's* Sense and Sensibility. *Her appearance opposite Leonardo DiCaprio in James Cameron's* Titanic *made her an international star. She is married to director Sam Mendes (*American Beauty*) and has two children.*

IT'S THE FEMALE'S privilege to experiment. We get to express ourselves however we want. In my family of three girls and a boy, it was all about laughter and tears, catfights, playing, adventures, and experimenting.

We fought over clothes, even underwear, and who had the newest item of clothing and how quickly I was going to be able to fit into it so that I could borrow it too. There was a lot of dressing up as well. We'd dress up and choreograph dances, choosing crazy pieces of music to make up silly old dances to perform in our tiny garden for my mum and our neighbor. As soon as my younger brother could walk, I began tying head scarves on him, painting his cheeks with great brown circles of cocoa powder mixed with saliva, putting big gold hoop earrings on him to make him a gypsy. Incredibly, he's turned out sort of sane and normal, as heterosexual as they come, and with a wonderful understanding of women.

We girls were quite tomboyish, allowed to behave like boys, so we had that privilege, whereas often with boys they are questioned if they behave like girls. People say, "Oh, God, which way are they going to go?" That's tremendously unfair for boys and men, to be expected to be brave and bold and not to cry in front of others, particularly not in front of women. I've always thought of that as a great tragedy. Whenever I have met men who have been open with their emotions and who cry when they are moved by something or who cry when they're sad or cry when they're happy, I find that to be a particularly touching quality. I imagine it must be a tremendous relief for men when they are allowed to do that, allowed to express themselves.

If I'm in my brother's company, and I've gotten dressed to go out, and he sees me looking at myself in the mirror, he'll say, "No, your bum does not look big in that." He's able to sort of read my mind. This "Does my bum look fat?" concept comes from the media. There's an image that is painted of celebrities, models, and actresses who are in these glossy magazines. An image that these people are perfect and have these perfect shapes. It's an idea of perfection that I truly believe does not exist.

What is perfect? Nothing is perfect. You're only as happy as you feel. And that is a tremendously important thing for young women—to feel good about themselves, despite all the pressure from not just the movies but these magazines. The thing that drives me absolutely insane is that in every single cover image of a model or an actress we're covered in makeup, our hair has been worked on for two hours, we're sucking in our stomachs and holding our heads in a certain way to make our jawline look clean. Even if that hasn't happened, the photographer has taken the digital image and erased certain parts of you or shaved three inches off your hips on each side. Then these poor young girls go and buy these magazines and think, *Well, I want to look like her.* Except the person they want to look like doesn't actually look like that at all.

I am so appalled by the MTV program *I Want a Famous Face.* The second or the third show was about a girl who wanted to look like me. Initially I was intrigued. I sat down to watch, and within minutes I started to cry. This girl was having parts of her stomach cut away. I could not believe what she was putting herself through. I thought, *I am powerless. I am more powerless right now than I have ever been in my life.*

This girl wants to look like me, but she doesn't know me, she doesn't know what I really look like. She wanted these pert, full breasts. I've nursed two children. My breasts are not pert and full and high at all. Gravity takes its toll when you've been nursing and as time goes by. That's just what happens to the female form. This girl had all these magazine covers that I was on. She'd been watching movies that I was in, and she wanted to look like me. I was heartbroken for her. I was heartbroken because she had been so absorbed and consumed by this image of perfection that's been painted by magazines and movies.

It often takes two hours to set up the right lighting for an actress when she has a nude scene or even if she's scantily clad. This girl was talking about the sequence in *Titanic* when Jack draws Rose's portrait while she's lying naked on the chaise. I was twenty-one years old at the time, and I ate almost nothing prior to that scene because I was so terrified. It was a very uncomfortable experience for me. Thank God, I had Leo, who by that point had become a very good friend. I didn't feel uncomfortable with him, but a movie crew is made up of men standing around. You just know that they're all looking at your breasts. It's a very humiliating experience, but at the same time two to three hours of lighting had gone on to make me look good. It's heartbreaking to me that women watch these images and say, "I want to look like that" or "How come she gets to look so perfect?" It's just horrendous.

If that girl who wanted to look like me walked into my apartment, I'd show her how I feel. I would say, "Stand there. Don't move." I would strip off, and I would say, "This is the real me. I do not have six-pack abs. I do not have a toned ass. I do not have pert breasts. I do not have a flat stomach. I have cellulite." I would want to shout, "This is the real me!" Really, I'm not that hot. I do not have a perfect body at all.

I'm lucky, because I have a relationship that I am incredibly happy in and I'm old enough now to be comfortable with myself. I've gone through those teenage years of neurosis and fear when you question yourself. When you want to look great. When you want to be loved and you think that being loved means looking wonderful. That's the true tragedy of those teenage years, that women seem to feel that in order to be loved, to have a relationship with a man, they have to look good. That's the thing that is so heartbreaking.

I was fifteen or sixteen when I started acting and being paid for it. Doing little jobs, not much, and I was just myself. Working with other actresses who were very slim, very attractive, who had wonderful long blond hair. I was always the slightly chubby misfit with very big feet and not particularly wonderful hair. I started to feel very self-conscious. I was heavy as a teenager. I was very heavy, and I lost some weight in a sensible way. But that was because I wanted to be more comfortable in my own skin. I got to a weight that felt comfortable to me.

But then it's the world of movies, and the pressure is on to look good and to be the show pony. After I did *Titanic*, I remember thinking, *Now, hang on a second. I feel good about myself. I feel comfortable with my body.* But I still knew that I wasn't as slim as some actresses are. I thought, *Well, I'm not going to do that anymore. I'm not going to crucify myself or not eat enough just to be smaller. I'm actually going to come out there and say, "Listen, I was in the highest-grossing movie ever made, and I'm not a stick."*

I really felt now's my chance. Maybe I could say something about this. Maybe I could tell young women that you don't have to be skinny and emaciated to actually achieve your goals. I never really had the goal to be a movie star. I just knew that I wanted to act and do the things that I loved most in the world. And here I was doing it. I was being successful at it, and I wasn't starving myself. That was a big deal for me.

I was able to fully appreciate my curves as I got a little bit older. I started to realize that having normal-size breasts was actually not a bad thing. It turned out that men quite liked that too, which was also a surprise to me, because I had convinced myself that all men wanted were slim women. It was a revelation. I think that's changing now, and some ads have models that are almost normal-size.

I'm a big believer in having your group of girls, in my case two or three very good girlfriends. When I've had tough times, I fall back on them. There are things I've gone through in my life that I would not have been able to understand as well were it not for the kind of coaching and guidance I got from my girlfriends, things I would have done differently if left to my own devices. I'll phone and talk to them for ages, or meet for a walk or dinner or coffee. It's a place I can go where I'm not judged. Where I can sit and cry for two hours if I feel like it. Where I can come out with absolute bullshit that doesn't make sense and they're not going to tell me I'm being stupid.

Any new relationship that I have had from the age of fifteen until the point that I married Sam, my husband, I would always sit down with my girlfriends, and say, "Oh, you know he does this thing, and he does that thing," and discuss quite intimate stuff. About five years ago, I was talking to a male friend who was having trouble in a relationship. I told him he needed to talk to a guy, because I could only help so far. I'm not a man. I don't know what that feels like. He said to me, "No, guys don't do that." I came to realize that men don't discuss the finer, more intimate, even sexual details of their relationships with a male friend. I can't imagine not being able to do that. That is very much the female privilege. For men, they're expected to deal with it and figure it out on their own. That's really sad, I think. It's great being a girl.

Kate Winslet

Carole L. Glickfeld

As a child of deaf adults, Carole L. Glickfeld has said that American Sign Language was practically her first language. She won the Flannery O'Connor Award for Short Fiction with Useful Gifts *(1989), a collection of interrelated short stories about a character named Ruthie Zimmer, the youngest child of deaf-mute parents. Her first novel,* Swimming Toward the Ocean *(2001), garnered highly favorable reviews and brought her a Washington State 2002 Book Award. Carole lives in Seattle, where she has taught creative writing at the University of Washington.*

As I WAS GROWING UP, the gender lines in my family were clearly drawn. My father went to work to support us. My mother took care of the kids and everything that had to do with the apartment. Although at age seven I aspired to be a teacher, somehow I knew that I'd teach only until I got married, whereupon my real future would begin. I would employ my talents to dust, wash, iron, cook, and in general keep an apartment clean and orderly. I would behave frugally and practically, especially when buying gifts for birthdays and Hanukkah, the kind my mother had bought for us, useful gifts such as white cotton underwear, socks, sturdy shoes.

So it was an education to encounter Dot, the mother of my new best friend, Leilani, and her stepbrother, Buster (I've changed their names, but not much else). They had recently moved into a ground-floor apartment in my building in Inwood (in the upper part of Manhattan) and from the get-go began to change my perspective on what it meant to be female.

Instead of wearing housedresses as my mother did at home (printed cotton, tidy but sexless), Dot wore sweaters or halter tops and slacks that showed off her curvy, statuesque figure. Whereas my mother's brown hair was pulled back on the sides, the ends rolled neatly in a kind of back-of-the-neck pageboy, Dot's hair was a pile of swirls, a carefully created effect of dishabille—and her hair changed color every couple of weeks: Maureen O'Hara red, Betty Grable blond.

At that time, divorce was mainly the province of the rich and/or famous. Real women could not afford either the divorce itself or a future without their husband's financial support, especially for their offspring. Dot, mother of two, had been divorced twice. What the neighbors took for "looseness," I took for bravery. In our tenement, there were no other mothers without a husband in residence, no other mothers who worked outside the home. There were, however, two women who lived together and had outside jobs, though they were suspected of being lesbians. Dot was brazenly heterosexual. She had a boyfriend with whom she openly smooched. I'd never even seen my parents kiss on the lips or embrace more than a polite second or two. Yet there were Dot and her boyfriend, rolling around on the floor in each other's arms, previewing the beach scene in *From Here to Eternity.* I'd never seen my mother even *sit* on the floor.

My mother dust-mopped our floors daily. Dot, she acknowledged, didn't have time to dust, which is why she viewed Dot's place as a germ-ridden zone and discouraged me from eating there. Dot worked nights as a hatcheck girl in a nightclub and left the dust-mopping to her son. It was eye-opening to see Buster—a fan of war games—do the dishes. Dishes needed washing, even if no one was cooking. My father thought it would make Buster a "fairy."

In our family, sandwiches were only an expedient, something my mother made for my father to take to work. Leilani and Buster lived on sandwiches of unidentifiable lunch meats, mustard, and mayo. Leilani knew how to slit open little cardboard boxes of cereal and pour the milk into them. Buster ate sticks of butter out of the wrapper. To them, "real meals" consisted of takeout. Dot brought home cartons of macaroni and potato salad or Chinese food she dished up onto Melmac plates. She took us to real restaurants, the kind that served American food, and left large tips. Who said women had to cook?

Dot spent most of her time at home fixing herself up: When she wasn't dyeing her hair a different color or polishing her fingernails or toenails, she was in a filmy robe and a towel turban, applying creams, lotions, or mud packs, tweezing her eyebrows, creating a mole slightly below and to the side of her bottom lip. "Men like women to fix themselves up," she told me, "but if you let them see you do it, it defeats the whole purpose."

By making me conscious of her, Dot made me conscious of myself—beyond the role I was destined to play because of my gender. My mother discouraged my sister and me from looking at ourselves in the mirror, telling us that it would make us homely. By contrast, Dot had installed large light globes all around the bathroom mirror and used a huge magnifying mirror besides. My mother never (and I mean never) complimented me. I took this to mean that I was hopelessly ugly, never more so than when next to Leilani's olive-skinned beauty (her father was Hawaiian-Chinese). Dutifully, my mother braided my hair each morning, but occasionally Dot would undo the tight pigtails and style my hair. With a few magical smushes, she'd make me look . . . well, like someone else. She would hold my face in her hands and, with her long nails, puncture and squeeze my pimples. I was so thrilled at the attention I hardly minded the pain.

MY ALL-TIME FAVORITE gift of my childhood was the pink model's hatbox Dot gave me, with my name written in large gold script across it. It was hardly a practical gift. It spoke to vanity. It flaunted. It was the perfect gift for a little girl in America.

The sixties and seventies changed Americans' perceptions of women; we evolved to unisex. At least for a time.

Nowadays when I see push-up bras, bra straps, and camisoles on display, or the tops of thongs on young women as they lean forward, sitting or standing, or purses that make a statement akin to a model's hatbox, I see women unabashedly expressing their female selves the way Dot did in the fifties. Working outside the home full-time, a single mom, she was a harbinger of women to come in the twenty-first century. And I have to wonder, what will *their* daughters (or daughters' friends) be like when they grow up?

Carole L Glickfeld

Eva Hoffman

Eva Hoffman is the author of Lost in Translation: A Life in a
New Language *(1989),* Shtetl: The Life and Death of a Small
Town in the World of Polish Jewry *(1997), and* Exit into History: A Journey Through the New Eastern Europe *(1993).*
Emigrating to Canada from Poland as a teen in 1959, she continued
her education in the United States, receiving her Ph.D. in English
and American literature from Harvard. She was a critic and senior ed-
itor at the New York Times *from 1979 to 1990 and has written*
articles on cultural and political subjects for the Atlantic Monthly,
the Yale Review, *and other publications. Her debut novel,* The Secret *(2002), is about a teenager who discovers that her birth in 2005*
was achieved through cloning. Hoffman has received numerous grants
and awards, including a Guggenheim Fellowship, a prize from the
American Academy of Arts and Letters, and a Whiting Award for
Writing.

MY FATHER SAID HE wanted me to be "a man from the establishment." That was the exact phrase, and even as I registered its
linguistic irregularity with amusement (he meant "an estab-

lished man"), it entered my mind as half flattering compliment, half hurtful spur.

My father was speaking in his idiosyncratic English, which he had learned late in life, after we emigrated to Canada. He was forty-eight years old, a brilliant man who had no profession or formal education. He never made good in Canada, never became "a man from the establishment" himself.

On this occasion, my father had a specific suggestion: He wanted me to call Zbigniew Brzezinski, newly made national security adviser to President Carter, and announce myself as someone who could be of help. After all, Brzezinski was Polish too, and I was at Harvard and so was a person of substance, if not yet a member of Washington's inner circle.

A man from the establishment. The masculine form was simply a mistake, but at the same time it was telling: My father wanted me to achieve things in the world that would have been considered conventionally masculine. Be a doctor, be a lawyer, ride that bicycle faster. And all right, so you work for the *New York Times,* but why can't you be on the front page?

My father did not have a very good idea of how to go about actually accomplishing such things in the confusing and tantalizing New World. His notion that I could call the president's counselor out of the blue had a touch of the old folklore about it, the peasant going to the czar, the powerless receiving the magic touch of power.

But how was I going to square all those contradictory expectations within myself? How was I going to be both woman and man?

There is no denying that psychologically this was a struggle that had its costs. I kept trying to put myself in every position: Be supportive, soothing, empathetic; be ambitious, adventurous, self-propelling. There was also the immigrant child's—immigrant daughter's—guilt for going so much further in the world than her parents, so much further than her father. The guilt was often oppressive, and I still feel the sadness of it acutely. Neither my father nor my mother had half—or one-tenth—the chances that were given to me.

And yet it helped me too, to have my father's great expectations spurring me on. It helped me not to have to think of myself as exclusively "womanly," in those now outmoded and constricting categories. It helped me fight hard for my professional and creative life. I think I would have shriveled and shrunk without it, would have been diminished to half of what I really was. My father was hardly a feminist, and yet he had dreams on behalf of his daughter that he would have had on behalf of his son—on behalf, if he only could, of himself. Of course, I did not call Zbigniew Brzezinski. By then I was savvy enough to know that this was not the way to go about pursuing the opportunities that the New World had to offer. But all in all, as I remember that funny, poignant, incongruous conversation with my father, even as I am struck again by its many ambiguities, I am also touched by it—and feel a touch of gratitude.

Eva Hoffman

Judy Martin

An Emmy Award–winning television journalist and national radio reporter, Judy Martin has a passion for covering social issues, humanitarian causes, and business. She has contributed to National Public Radio, the Marketplace Report, *and the* World Vision Report. *For more than a decade, she has maintained her relationship with the News 12 Television Networks as an anchor. Judy is a recipient of the National Press Foundation Economic Fellowship, an Associated Press Award for Feature Reporting, numerous New York Press Club Awards, and a New York Emmy for Outstanding Coverage of a Breaking News Story. Judy is a hospice volunteer and also works with children with HIV/AIDS in a program with the River Fund New York. Since reporting and volunteering in the aftermath of the September 11 terror attacks, she has been facilitating workshops called PRACTICAL CHAOS® on conquering chaos in life and work.*

BRIGHT RED LIPSTICK. Flowing Farrah Fawcett hair. It was the look I mimicked as the "new" me. Skintight jeans graced my little body and spiked heels gave me just the rise I needed to make me taller and so much bigger than life in my little, newly teenage head. This was the look that I'd play around with when trying to impress the boys in school. To me it was powerful, and would demonstrate my prowess as a woman of the world who had suddenly emerged on the junior high scene.

Turning thirteen was more of a "becoming thirteen," rather than just a small turning point in my relatively short existence and meager experience. I was becoming a woman, and the rich fruit of that journey was not lost on my mom. The truth is that my mom's keen, discerning, but watchful eye would challenge my inner and outer view of myself throughout my growth as a woman, but especially at this vulnerable age. I was now becoming an adult, with all the outward appearances and attitudes that I perceived as coming along with age. It was the kind of stuff I had seen on television. The *Charlie's Angels* television series had formed the image of the power of the feminine to some degree. The angels were strong-minded, intelligent, but beautiful and sexy women. I would be like them. I was now becoming an adult who could make her own decisions. An adult who could now perhaps even get a kiss from my childhood sweetheart, Timmy. An adult who would finally turn the heads of those I had crushes on in junior high. Finally I might make my life complete with a boyfriend. Acceptance.

Much to my disappointment, which I would now describe clearly as grace, my mom had a different view of my new image and my thoughts of where it would take me in my growth as a woman.

At thirteen, I was in a community-theater skit taken

from the musical *Grease*. I was playing the sexy, tough siren. I donned a revealing dress with spaghetti straps. I wore lots of makeup, which evidently covered my innocence and aged me—and put the fear of God into my mom's eyes and demeanor, as I would soon learn.

I had pulled off the skit, I thought, with great presence and sophistication. Timmy was in the audience, and when the performance ended that evening, I removed myself from my parental units and headed in the direction of Timmy so he could check me out. Much to my dismay, he was thoroughly uninterested. It broke my heart. My apparent sexy disposition and new look didn't so much as turn his head. I was thirteen and he was sixteen. I was crushed.

Coming home that evening, I was feeling rather down. My mom was quiet when we walked through the door. I hadn't received the praise from her that I had expected, and Timmy had rejected me. My new image and performance had received a standing ovation from the audience. But that was a fleeting experience. My mom and Timmy were the people I wanted to impress the most, and in that respect I had fallen flat.

Preparing for hitting the sack that night, I found on my bed a letter that my mom had written while I'd been finishing up homework and watching television.

My Dear Love Judy,

You are a lovely, talented, intelligent, creative woman. Did you know that your body is sacred? That not only you live in your body but that God lives there too? Last night rather than use your truly wonderful gift of acting, you simply showed your body. Your body is beautiful, Judy. But that's not a reason to make it a showpiece. I know you are a little girl, and you probably saw something like this on TV. Please hear me—please be sensible as you grow, and treat your body with respect.

I am not angry with you. I love you and want to share that you don't have to impress anyone but your own inner soul. To do that you have to respect yourself and not worry about impressing others, like Timmy. It's faulty thinking to think deep down that you're nobody until somebody loves you.

As a child I learned from society that a woman comes into her power when loved and admired by a man. This love means approval. What if it doesn't work out? The way to avoid that is to know that you don't need a man's approval to complete you. You don't need anyone else's approval.

Judy dear, you have so much to offer. You can't love another fully unless you love yourself first, and enough.

My mom wrote about becoming an adult and all that went along with it. About how life would unfold and my strength would reveal itself in the form of my feminine power in time. About how to enjoy the emergence of my womanhood slowly. About how nothing outside of me would ever complete me. About how the love of a man can be a quick fix or a source of mutual growth and respect as human beings. The letter has been read over the last thirty years again and again, and each time I get closer and closer to my final destination. Peace within my soul and myself. Acceptance of who I am, with all the flaws and all the beauty.

Judy Martin

Zane

Zane is the New York Times *bestselling author of nine books of erotic fiction:* Afterburn, Skyscraper, Nervous, The Sisters of APF, Gettin' Buck Wild: The Sex Chronicles 2, The Heat Seekers, Shame on It All, Addicted, *and* The Sex Chronicles: Shattering the Myth. *She is the publisher of Strebor Books International, an imprint of Atria/Simon & Schuster, under which she publishes more than fifty authors. She has been published in many languages and has sold more than four million books.*

LIKE MOST FEMALES', my youth was full of both pleasant and disturbing experiences. There are some things in life you can be prepared for through lengthy discussions with one or both parents. They can explain why your breasts are suddenly poking out of your chest and console you when you get your first menstrual cycle. However, even with the longest talks known to man, they cannot prepare you for other things. Sure, we can have sex education in school, but does sex really ever feel the way we expect it to the first few times? Can we really understand that the first time a boy dumps us for a prettier or more popular girl, our hearts will literally feel like they have broken?

Can we really understand that no matter how hard we try to make a relationship work, sometimes matters are just beyond our control?

I have so many friends and family members who have fallen into the same trap, allowing themselves to be defined by a man. Thank goodness I had a strong mother and grandmother, both women married for more than fifty years but totally independent and goal-oriented at the same time. If not for them, I might have fallen into the same trap. I wish there could be a public-service announcement aired daily and internationally, one that simply states, "Young ladies, concentrate on developing yourself first, and the relationships with men will follow!"

I recently had a conversation with a relative whose husband was throwing a tantrum because she wanted to come and visit me for a few days from out of town. She planned to make it easy for him—a quick trip, and she would bring the kids with her—but still he just didn't want her to go. She asked me if she should apologize to him. I told her that she'd better not, because she has absolutely nothing to apologize for. She deserves a life, independent of her one with him, and he just has to accept it. The days of women rubbing their husband's feet at night, fixing their dinner plates, and doing their laundry need to end. I am not blaming the women that still play into that philosophy. It is usually a learned behavior. My older aunts always talk about how we younger women walk away from marriages too quickly, and they seemingly brag about all they endured in the name of love in lengthy marriages. No, thank you! One of my favorite quotes of all time came from Steven Biko, the man Denzel Washington so powerfully portrayed in *Cry Freedom*: "The greatest weapon the oppressor ever has is the mind of the oppressed." Once your mind is convinced of something, the battle is over.

That brings me to the other thing I would like all females to know. Sexual satisfaction should always be mutual and not just a male thing. It is ironic that I have grown up to write erotic fiction, because, like most females, I was told that good girls did not do certain things. I was taught to be sexually repressed and understand that men are entitled to sexual gratification 100 percent of the time, while I should only hope to luck out every once in a while and have an actual orgasm. I am so glad that I figured it out back in the mid-1990s. I am entitled to satisfaction each and every time I have sex, or it is not even worth my time.

It amazes me that some people still assume that I am a man because I write sex books. They cannot seem to get over the fact that a woman would be so candid when it comes to writing about sex. There are millions of women out there who fantasize about sex the way I do. That is what I love so much about my characters. They are the women so many of us would be if we did not have responsibilities and could throw caution to the wind and just live out our desires. They are empowered and liberated. So am I.

Suzanne Somers

Originally Suzanne Marie Mahoney, one of four children born to Frank and Marion Mahoney, the girl who became Suzanne Somers showed an early love for the arts and was active in her school's theatre program. She worked in television and films, starring in the hit TV series Three's Company. *After leaving that series, she worked extensively in Las Vegas, winning the Las Vegas Entertainer of the Year Award in 1984. She's also won a People's Choice Award as Best Female Performer in a New TV Series in 1992, a National Council on Alcoholism Humanitarian Award that same year, and, in 1993, the National Association of American Drug Counselors President's Award.*

I DON'T REMEMBER having my own life as a girl. Every fiber of my being was preoccupied with the troubles going on in our home. My father was a raging alcoholic, and that was my focus. I felt that if I could just somehow be a better daughter, then he wouldn't have to drink so much. In my child's mind, I somehow felt it was my fault, and that became my burden.

To understand the world from a child's point of view, lie on the floor and look up at an adult. That should give you some idea of the power we wield over our children. My mother was afraid of my father, and so I in turn was also.

My father criticized my developing body until I was mortified to be walking around in it. I didn't realize then that this was his ploy to keep me bound to him. Alcoholics are bullies, and they need to keep those around them in a state of fear so they won't leave. I felt paralyzed all the time. This overwhelming fear made it impossible for me to learn and develop normally. I was terribly insecure and felt that I didn't deserve to inhabit the little space I occupied on this earth.

The daily violence of my early life forced me out of his home; anything would be better than staying with all that craziness. But I was unprepared for life on my own. Teenage pregnancy, teenage divorce, and being financially destitute added to my already overloaded sense of shame and low self-worth. I had been told by my father since birth that I was "stupid, worthless, and hopeless," and that is what I believed.

But I had dreams. When I still lived in my father's house, we would have to hide in the upstairs closet most nights, when his raging would become life-threatening, and it was in that closet that I would escape into fantasies of being on a stage, where life was beautiful. In those dreams, my mother would be in the front row, and she was finally happy and not afraid. I wanted to save us, and in my fantasies I could. In my daydreams, I was powerful. As an adult, I now realize that those dreams and fantasies were my salvation. The seed was planted, and somehow, without understanding, I was emerging.

One night, my father attacked my mother and me, and it was seeing her on the floor, hurt and crying, that made me say, "NO MORE." With that, I took my tennis racquet and hit him with such intensity that I knocked him unconscious. Blood squirted out of his head like a geyser; I screamed hysterically, and my mother dragged him out into the car and to the hospital. I was left alone in that house of horrors, with blood everywhere, with all the craziness, with thoughts of ending my own life. I wanted out, I wanted to be normal.

Sometimes it is in the moments of greatest despair that we see the light of hope. After this incident, my father backed off. He kept drinking, he kept staring at me like he was going to kill me if he ever got me alone, but he never touched me again. In time, I realized that he was afraid of me, that he couldn't bully me anymore. I had had enough. In that motion of raising that tennis racquet over my head, I had taken my power.

This incident shaped me as a person. Not that I am proud of resorting to such violence, but as human beings we can be pushed only so far, and then we choose either to be victims or to fight back. I chose to fight back.

As a woman today, I am now a fighter. A gentle warrior, but nonetheless don't mess with me. I am not violent—it's not my nature—but I cannot tolerate being treated without respect.

My dreams ultimately transported me into my reality, where I now live my life on a stage. The stage is a metaphor, of course, but my books, my television career, nightclubs, lecturing, my one-woman Broadway show, the brand I have established as a businesswoman—they all tell me that it doesn't matter where you come from or what has happened to you in your life. We all have the power to change our lives. Inside each one of us is the human spirit, pure joy and love, and no matter who tries to knock it out of us, the spirit can endure and overcome.

Today I find myself, in some ways, grateful for my father. He was the person who caused me the most pain in my life, and as a result of the experience of being his daughter, he is the person from whom I learned the most.

That is life. I now know that the silver lining resides inside each one of us, but it is up to each of us as individuals to find it in ourselves. I wouldn't trade my childhood. Because of it, I have grown into a woman who can hold her head up high. I feel good about myself and the part I play in the connectedness of all living things. I have done the work to change my life, and the process is ongoing. We are all here together to help one another on our journey of evolution to be the best person we can be. Life takes work. But what you put into it is the reward you get back. Growing up female has become my advantage. The nature of the male is to fight back; rarely does the female think she can, but in doing so, I learned that you take what life gives you and find a way to make it your opportunity. I fought back, not only physically but emotionally. I have fought for every accomplishment, every relationship of meaning, and I have not let obstacles big or small keep me down. Because of it, I wake up each day happy, grateful to be alive, grateful to be me, grateful for the privilege of growing up female.

Kate Michelman

Kate Michelman has been a leader in the pro-choice movement throughout much of her career, working from 1985 to 2004 as president of NARAL Pro-Choice America. Before that, she was the executive director of Planned Parenthood in Harrisburg, Pennsylvania, and a fellow at the John F. Kennedy School of Government's Institute of Politics at Harvard University. Vanity Fair *magazine named her one of America's 200 Women Legends, Leaders, and Trailblazers, and* Washingtonian *magazine named her one of the capital's hundred most powerful women. She is the author of* With Liberty and Justice for All: A Life Spent Protecting the Right to Choose.

IN 1970, I WAS A YOUNG MOTHER and homemaker when my husband suddenly left me. I learned that I was pregnant shortly after and began a quest for a safe hospital abortion. My story is a portrait of the indignities and humiliation women suffered as they sought to make responsible reproductive choices.

I grew up in the 1950s, when the role of women centered on the family. I came from a close family, so I readily accepted that role. Like many women of my generation, I hoped to get married, have children, and own a home.

By 1970, I was married to a man who was pursuing his career as a college professor, and I had had three wonderful daughters in three years. We were struggling financially, but were able to scrape together the down payment on our first home. I hoped to work in the field of child development, but that was for the future. My daughters were my priority. My life was my family.

One night, my husband never came home. I was sure something terrible had happened to him. I called the police, to no avail. The next morning, my husband walked in the door and announced that he was in love with someone else and was leaving me. Then he was gone. It was not a gradual separation. It was an abrupt, dramatic break. He also walked out of my daughters' lives.

I was devastated. I was frightened. My self-esteem was destroyed. Suddenly my world had collapsed. My vision of life had shattered. I was terrified—terrified of being alone. Terrified of having sole responsibility for my daughters. Terrified of having to provide for my family. I was shaken to the core.

My daughters were also hurt. They too felt rejected. I was worried they would be permanently scarred. How could I alone provide all they needed and deserved? I felt that I had failed them. I blamed myself for their suffering.

A few weeks later, I discovered I was pregnant again. This news further devastated me. Another child would cause an unmanageable crisis and destroy my family's ability to cope. I felt as if the very survival of my family were at stake.

I alone had to meet my children's every need—financial,

emotional, and physical. I had no money, job, or car. I had to ask friends to drive me to the market. The five-and-dime store refused to give me a charge account to buy school supplies for my children. I couldn't make the mortgage payments, and I had to sell my home and move into a small rental town house. My family was forced onto welfare. Facing another pregnancy was more than I could handle.

I never thought that I would have to make the decision about whether to have an abortion. I was raised in a Catholic family, and I was a devout Catholic at the time. For many years, I strictly followed the church's teachings. I even believed that using birth control was a sin.

Abortion was a crime. The very word evoked fear and shame. People didn't talk about it, and I couldn't even discuss it with my mother or sister. I was forced to struggle with this decision alone.

Deciding whether to have an abortion was one of the most difficult and complex decisions of my life. It challenged every religious, moral, and ethical belief I held. I had to weigh and balance the overwhelming moral responsibility to care for, feed, and nurture my daughters against my responsibility to the developing life within me. I had to take responsibility, not only for my own life but also for the lives of my daughters. In the end, I made what I believe was one of the most moral decisions of my life. I decided to have an abortion.

There were only two ways to have an abortion then—in the back alleys or in the hospital. To have a therapeutic abortion in the hospital, you had to persuade a panel of doctors to grant you one. Some women had to prove that their lives were in danger. I had to convince the all-male panel that I was not capable of raising another child, that I was unfit to be a mother—even though I had three daughters. They asked intimate questions about my life—about my marriage, what kind of wife I was, what kind of mother I was. I felt ashamed and degraded—and more worthless than ever. The only alternative to a hospital procedure was an illegal abortion. Someone gave me the phone number of an illegal abortionist, which I carried with me at all times. I was prepared to risk my life if I had no other choice.

The hospital panel finally granted me permission to have the abortion. I was relieved. I arranged to have a friend care for my children and went to the hospital. There I faced one more indignity. A nurse told me they had forgotten about another legal requirement—I had to get the written permission of my husband. I explained that my husband had left me. She said it was the law and that if I did not comply, I could not have the abortion.

It never occurred to me to try to get around this law. I did what I was told. I got dressed and left the hospital to search for the man who had deserted me. It was just one more humiliation.

He gave his permission, and I had the abortion. When I woke up in the recovery room, I was glad that it was over, but I felt such overwhelming loneliness. I felt like a failure. My husband was gone, my family was in turmoil, and I was worried about the future.

I slowly put the pieces of my life together. It took me quite a while to restore my sense of worth and to meet the various obligations and responsibilities of my family. Eventually my daughters and I recovered and moved on. I completed my degree and found part-time work in the field of child development.

My experience with abortion, as well as my work with developmentally disabled children, taught me how important reproductive choices are to a woman's life and to the well-being of her family. That I was forced to consider risking my life in order to make a responsible decision for my family shocked and profoundly changed me.

Roe v. Wade was decided three years after my abortion. It felt like a retroactive recognition of my decision. The ruling from the highest court in the land provided an affirmation that my decision was indeed mine, and mine alone, to make.

Within several years of *Roe,* I decided to devote my life's work to ensuring that no woman would ever again have to face the indignities I faced or risk her life when making reproductive choices. Today women no longer have to endure back-alley abortions. But for the most vulnerable women— the young, the poor, women of color, women living in rural communities—the freedom to choose has become virtually a right in name only. And *Roe v. Wade* hangs by a slender thread in the Supreme Court, which is one or two votes away from turning back the clock on a woman's fundamental right to choose.

I will continue to make the daily fight to secure the

freedom to choose for all women, including my three daughters and their children. It is for them that I persist in this fight. It is for them that I give voice to my story—so that they never have to face the shame, degradation, and humiliation that I and countless other women suffered when taking personal responsibility for our lives and for our families.

Kate Michelman

Jyl Lynn Felman

Jyl Lynn Felman, author, performance artist, and lawyer, taught women's studies at Brandeis University for eight years. Currently she teaches at the University of Massachusetts, Amherst, where she was nominated in fall 2005 for the Distinguished Professor Award. Her memoir, Cravings, *is about growing up Jewish and female (1997), and* Hot Chicken Wings, *short stories, was a 1993 Lambda Literary Finalist.* If Only I'd Been Born a Kosher Chicken, *her autobiographical, one woman show aired (1997) on C-SPAN's* Performance *series. She's appeared at more than twenty-five universities in England, Canada, the United States, Australia, Cuba, and the Czech Republic and has been featured on radio, TV, the BBC, and NPR.* Never a Dull Moment: Teaching and the Art of Performance *was published (2001) to wide acclaim.* Performing Cultural Rituals: Public, Private, and Peculiar *is forthcoming in fall 2006. Currently, Felman is touring with three new autobiographical performance pieces:* Burning in Cuba, Terri Schiavo, Inc., *and* Silicone Valley, *which is about the impact of breast cancer on desire in long-term relationships. See www.jyllynnfelman.com for her complete biography.*

THE PROBLEM with my mother's dying is not so much that she died, but that she died without telling me how to cook a chicken. If I could cook a chicken the way my mother did, I could have her with me always, or so I imagine. Whenever I want to talk to my mother, I go to the kosher butcher and I cook that chicken until my mother appears alive and well before me. So strong is the smell of the roasting chicken in my mind that I feel my mother coming into the room this very minute.

MY MOTHER WASHED us both in the same kitchen sink. I don't know who came first, the baby or the bird. First I am on the counter watching, then I am in the sink splashing. My mother washes me the way she washes her kosher *Shabbas* chicken breasts. Slow and methodical, as though praying, she lifts my small right arm; she lifts the wings of the chicken; and scrubs all the way up to where she cannot scrub anymore, to where the wing is attached to the body, the arm to the shoulder. Gently, she returns my short, stubby arms to the side of my plump body, which remains propped upright in the large kitchen sink. Automatically, my arms extend outward, eternally and forever reaching for her.

The cold wet chicken, washed and scrubbed, sits next to us on the counter. We're identical, the chicken and I, except for our heads and the feathers. The chicken has no head and I have no feathers. But I will have hair. Lots of body hair that my mother will religiously teach me to pluck and to shave until my adolescent body resembles a perfectly plucked, pale young bird waiting to be cooked to a hot, crisp, golden brown and served on the same sacred platter as my mother herself was before me.

At thirteen, I stand on the bimah and prepare to chant. I am also upstairs in the bathroom, alone in the terrifying wilderness of my adolescent femaleness. On my head is a white, silk yarmulke, held in place by two invisible bobby pins. For the first time in my life, I prepare my female self the exact same way she taught me in her kosher kitchen sink. *Borchu et Adonai hamvorach.* I look out at the congregation. My mother is crying. I look in the mirror; I inspect my face; my eyebrows are dark brown and very thick. *Baruch Adonai hamvorach laolam vaed.* I place the tweezers as close to the skin as possible to catch the root, so the hair won't ever grow back. *Baruch atah Adonai, Elohaynu melech haolam . . .* My parents are holding hands as I recite the third blessing in honor of being called to the Torah. And then I begin. Although my *haftorah* portion is long and difficult, I want it to last forever because I love the sonorous sounds of the mystical Hebrew letters. But I am surprised at how much it hurts to pull out a single hair, one at a time, out from under my pale, young skin. When I reach the final closing blessings, my voice is strong and full and I do not want to stop.

Only I am surprised at how much it hurts to shape my thick Ashkenazi eyebrows into small elegant, Anglo female arches. Then I remember the ice cubes that she soaks the chickens in, to keep them fresh and cold before the plucking, and how I used to watch her pluck out a long, hard particularly difficult feather without a single break. The congregation sings, *Mi chamocha baelim Adonai.* I return to the kitchen for ice cubes wrapped in terry cloth, which I hold diligently up to my adolescent brow. *Mi chamocha nedar bakodesh . . . Who is like unto thee, O most High, revered and praised, doing wonders?* I have no feeling above my eyes, but the frozen skin is finally ready for plucking.

These first female rituals have no prayers as I stand before the rabbi utterly proud of what I have accomplished. He places his hands above my head, *Yevarechecha Adonai . . .* He blesses my youthful passage into the adult community of Jews. I am alone in the bathroom now, and my eyes water as I watch the furrowed brow of my beloved ancestors disappear from my face forever. At the exact same moment that I become a bat mitzvah, I begin the complex process of preparing myself for rebirth into gentility. I complete these first female rites in silence, without the comfort of my mother or a single Hebrew *brocha.* The congregation rises, together we say, *Yisgadal, veyiskadash sh'mei rabah.* I have become a beloved daughter of the covenant, only the covenant is confusing. *Shema Yisrael Adonai eloheinu,* I love my people Israel, but I loathe my female self.

I am balanced precariously between the sink, the toilet, and the cold tile floor. I use my father's shaving cream to hide all traces of the hair growing up and down my legs. Slowly and methodically, I scrape the hair off each leg. I have to concentrate very hard so I don't cut myself. I stop to rinse out the thick tufts of hair stuck in the razor's edge. Then I inspect the quality of my work. The finished skin has to be completely smooth, as though there were never any thick brown hair covering my body. When I am finished shaving my legs, I raise my right arm and stare into the mirror. The hair under my arms is soft and there isn't very much there. At thirteen, I do not understand why I have to remove this hair too. As I glide the razor back and forth, I am aware of how tender my skin is and how raw it feels once all the hair is removed. Rinsing off the now clean space, I notice that the skin is turning red. And when I roll on the sticky, sweet-scented deodorant, it burns. But I lower my right arm, lift my left one, and begin again until I am fully plucked and have become my mother's chicken.

She shows me how to remove all traces of blood from the body. After soaking, there is salting. But the blood of the chicken accumulates under the wings and does not drain out into her spotless kosher sink. She roasts each chicken for hours, turning the thighs over and over, checking for unclean spots that do not disappear even in the stifling oven heat. With a single stroke of the hand and a silver spoon, she removes a spot of blood from the yolk of an imperfect egg. First she cracks each one separately into a glass bowl; if the yolk is clear, luminous, she adds it to another bowl. But whenever the blood spreads like tiny veins into the center of the bright yellow ball, she throws out the whole egg.

For my turn, I roll the egg slowly in between my palms; I learn to feel the blood pulsating right inside the center so I don't ever have to break it open. I learn that the sight of red blood on the food Jews eat is disgusting. Red juice from an undercooked chicken always makes me gag. I stop eating red meat. I eat all my food cooked well done. I do not tell my mother when I start to bleed. Instinctively, I keep my fe-maleness to myself.

When she finds out, she is furious. How long? I cannot remember. She is hurt. When was the first time? I do not remember. She is almost hysterical, but I cannot remember. I remember only that all signs of blood on the body must be removed. I wrap wads of cotton in toilet paper so thick that no one will ever guess what's inside. I clean myself the exact same way she cleans blood from the chickens in her sink. I soak and I salt, for hours at a time. For years, I will away my own femaleness. I do not spill for months in a row and then, when I do, it's just a spot, a small speck, easily removed, like the red spot floating in my mother's yolk.

Before I am born, I float in my mother's yolk and I am never hungry. Soon after I am born, the hunger begins. By seventeen, I am so hungry I do not know what to do with myself. All I can think about is food and how I cannot get enough.

At seventeen I leave the States for Israel. When I arrive, I cannot stop eating. I stuff myself the way my mother stuffs her kosher *Shabbas* chicken breasts. In Jerusalem, I cannot stop eating, waiting for the bus. I cannot stop eating halvah laced with green pistachios while *Mizrachi* women with olive skin soak in pools of turquoise water. I cannot stop eating whole figs with date jam spread on fresh Syrian bread while Sephardic women lie on heated marble slabs and close their eyes. I am never full. Jewish women bathe in ancient cleansing waters. I want to take my clothes off, but I cannot stop eating. Every Friday, I stay with an Orthodox family and light *Shabbas* candles as the sun sets. At night, I wander back alone from the center of the City, to where I live on Har Hatzofim. With my bus fare, I buy a kilo of jelly cookies. All I do in Israel at seventeen is eat. I tap a hunger so wide that I do not know what to do. I know that I will have to leave the country. There is no one to tell how hungry I have become because a hunger like this is forbidden. But I fall in love with Israel the way I will fall in love with a woman for the first time.

Alone, my mother flies to rescue me on an El Al jumbo jet. I have become a *knaydelach*, a dumpling, floating in the soup: a nice Jewish girl who doesn't say a word. But stuffed inside my mother's dumpling, swimming just below the surface, is a *vilde chaye*, a wild beast, waiting to get out. My mother takes the window seat, staring hard at me, her fat baby girl, drowning in the soup.

Flying back with her, I know that I have failed. She doesn't ask, and I cannot tell her, what exactly happened. That I fell in love. That I tapped a hunger I did not know I had. I have watched my mother eat and never gain a pound. She can eat and eat and eat, devour anything in sight, but I never see her body change. I never know what happens to all the food that she consumes. Mine shows on my body, right outside for everyone to see; but the food that she consumes disappears and is impossible to see.

When we arrive in the States, our covenant begins to break, mother to daughter, daughter to mother. We do not speak the words, but they float between us, growing larger day by day. Right after Pesach, like the first signs of spring, I start to grow all my body hair back again. *A Vilde Chaye.* She is mortified. It is so soft. She is horrified. I can't believe I ever shaved it off. A wild beast. I run my hands up and down my legs. And when I lift my arms, she turns her head away. She tells me that my body is disgusting. Not a nice Jewish girl, never seen or heard, who does not say a word. I thought my body was my own. More than her *knaydelach*, floating in the soup.

The covenant is broken; I've claimed my body as my own. But the silence floats between us, growing larger day by day. What my mother always feared is true. I grow up to be a stunning, raging, wild, forbidden *vilde chaye.* I did not ever want to leave my mother's *Shabbas* table; but in my twenties, she cannot set a place for me. I learn to close my eyes, light the candles, say the kiddush and the *motzi* by myself. But I cannot cook her chicken, so I cannot bring her home to me. And without my mother present, I cannot bear to eat her food.

I become a vegetarian, even though the food tastes strange and never smells the same. With other *vilde chayes*, I make a seder of my own. We become the red beets sprouting green leaves, sitting where the shank bones belong. We wash each other's hands as we pass the bowl around. But we cannot taste our mothers in the soup, and in their absence, we grow lame. How can I have my mother and myself? For years, we barely speak and in her absence, I grow tame. Only later do I know that her silence is her shame that she gave birth to me, who let my hair grow back. But I did not ever want to choose my mother or myself. And when we, *d'vilde chayes*, call forth our mothers' names: *emoteinu, Sarah, Rivkah, Rachel v Leah*, it is the first time I say my mother's name out loud.

I know that I have been cast out; that my hunger is the shame of both my mother and my people. There is no language I can speak as I shake my head in sorrow that I am not counted too. But I continue to look back, to remember who I am. *Im eshcachech Yerushalayim,* If I forget thee, Jerusalem. I know that my mother is waiting and looking back herself. Through her silence, she is praying that I reappear. Through my silence, I am praying for my mother to appear. At the seder table, my voice grows strong and clear. I learn that I must speak to those who do not want to hear, to my mother and my people. To say that I am your daughter too and cannot be forgotten or erased.

The truth is that I always was just like I am today. Only I didn't know, it wasn't possible, as I was growing up, to see any other way. For the longest time, I floated in the soup and didn't say a word. Then one day, I had to choose to leap right from the bowl. I came to understand that there are those of us who lead the way and those who like to follow. My mother was a follower who gave birth to a leader. This was not easy for my mother or myself. I did not choose to be a leader; it was chosen for me. But what I do not know is if my mother ever felt constrained, as I always did; if it was her choice to follow, or if she felt that she had no choice. Perhaps she was afraid to lead. This I'll never know. Yet this is how the cycle flows. In every generation, from follower to leader, from leader to follower.

All her life, my mother didn't understand what it meant to birth a *vilde chaye*. This was my aching disappointment. Before she died, I never had the chance to tell her that to lead like Moses or Deborah is to risk the people's wrath. That to be a *vilde chaye* is to live forever on the edge, with your life often at stake. I never had the chance to say out loud that I always needed her. My mother's grief at who I am is my deepest sorrow. More than anyone on earth, I wanted her to understand.

Sometimes, late at night, when I feel my people's wrath, I wonder, was she right? Is it better not ever to be seen or heard? A dumpling floating in the soup? Sometimes, late at night, I wonder, is it better just to be a nice Jewish girl rather than a *vilde chaye*? I always loved my mother and know that she loved me. The mistake I made is in her chicken that I never learned to cook. From the plucking to the soaking, from the salting to the stuffing, to the removal of the blood, we are bound to language and a common history. From the laws of kashrut to the sacred washing of the hands, it is in poultry that we are bound eternal, in our femaleness.

In my fantasy, I am born a kosher chicken with my mother's hands holding me. She washes me forever in her large kitchen sink. Cleaning my wings, she tells me not to change a thing, that she loves me just the way I am. On Friday afternoons, all her *Shabbas* friends come to see the baby soaking in the sink. They pinch and they poke, laughing at my teeny, tiny *polkies*. If only I was born a chicken, rather than a *vilde chaye*, there would be no painful separation from my mother or my people.

Near the end, I washed my mother's hands and feet. She couldn't talk, but she let me in that close. As I washed her legs and thighs, we made a silent, fragile peace; she the perfect *balaboosta*, and me, the stunning *vilde chaye*. But in my fantasy, I am born a kosher chicken. I sit forever plump and round, in the center of my mother's *Shabbas* table. When she lights the candles and closes her eyes, I am there forever, by my mother's side. She is there forever, by her daughter's side. We are together, at the *Shabbas* table, sitting side by side.

Jyl Lynn Felman

Rue McClanahan

*Born Eddi-Rue McClanahan in Healdton, Oklahoma, she gradu-
ated from the University of Tulsa with a degree in German and theatre arts. She began her career as a stage actress before being cast
by Norman Lear for roles in the TV series* All in the Family *and*
Maude. *She was nominated for both an Emmy and a Golden Globe
many times for her role as Blanche Devereaux in* The Golden
Girls. *She continues her acting career, which now includes a lecture,
called "Aging Gracefully," which she delivers to cancer support
groups.*

WHEN I WAS A LITTLE GIRL of seven or eight, I noticed that
the boys went out to play after lunch and the girls were kept in
to clear the table and wash and dry the dishes before being
excused. This was after every meal, three times a day.

Also, the men were fed at the "first table" and the women
served them, then ate after the men and boys had left the table.
There were dozens more examples of prejudice against us females, but this one was the first instance I noticed.

I experienced such prejudice every day of my life until

perhaps the early 1980s, with one exception. My second husband, Norman Hartweg, was completely liberated concerning women, and he always treated me as an equal. We remained best friends for forty years until his untimely death in 1994.

Ruth Clanahan

Julia Stiles

---

*Dividing her time between Columbia University and the film indus-
try, Julia Stiles continues to expand her repertoire by participating
in a variety of projects that showcase her growing abilities as a young
actress. A graduate of New York's Professional Children's School, she
won critical and popular attention for her role in the film* Ten Things
I Hate About You, *a variation on* The Taming of the Shrew.
*That led to several other films based on works by Shakespeare:
Michael Almereyda's* Hamlet *with Ethan Hawke, and* O, *a teen-
oriented adaptation of* Othello. *While attending school and starring
in films, she has also worked in Costa Rica with Habitat for Humanity.*

I GREW UP AS A CITY KID in New York, so from a very young
age I was taking the subway. It gave me an enormous amount
of freedom—I could go anywhere I wanted—which my
mother and grandmother did not experience while growing
up. But that sense of rebelliousness still flourished in them. The
women in my family have never bowed down to society's re-
strictions. During the 1950s, my grandmother was a housewife
in the suburbs, but when she turned fifty, she decided to start a

career in journalism. It was very pioneering for that time. And my mother is an incredible artist. When I was growing up, she had her studio in the basement of our building. She was always home when I was a child, but at night she'd go down to her studio and work for hours. Around four o'clock in the morning, I'd hear the freight elevator coming up and I'd know she was finished with her work. She worked really hard and she sacrificed so much for me—it was amazing how she incorporated her career into being an attentive, loving, and caring mother. If I ever needed her, all I had to do was ring that elevator bell and she'd come right up to see me.

I learned so much from my mother—not all of it consciously. Most of it was through osmosis, overhearing her conversations and watching the way she acted. She never directly preached to me, which is probably why her teaching was so effective. She gave me a sense of optimism and a feeling of empathy for other people. She has always had the ability to look at the positive side of things and find the positive side of people. When I was in elementary school in the eighties, she was very involved in the AIDS movement in Greenwich Village. She made ceramic funeral urns for gay men who were dying of AIDS. She poured her heart and soul into those urns, and by fostering relationships with these men she would find a way to personalize the urns, painting some aspect of their life on them—sometimes she would make little clay sculptures, almost like a bride and groom on the wedding cake, and put them on the top of the urns. She always tried to make it more of a joyful celebration of the relationship, rather than something more morose.

Recently I had a conversation with my mother in which she said to me, "Oh, you always look at the positive side of things." I said, "Well, I learned it from you." I have a job that puts me in a different country every two months. There's something kind of scary about that—you're not in your comfort zone. My mother equipped me to embrace that uneasy feeling, to find excitement in those adventures. Once, after spending six months working abroad, I went to Iceland for another job. When I first got there, I was feeling a bit homesick, and she came over to visit me. She found so much beauty in that country; it was so different from New York City. Observing the way she acted in this new environment shifted my perspective. After her visit, I started embracing the differences and began to appreciate and cherish my experience there.

I definitely feel I had more freedom growing up as a female than my mother did. When I was in high school, I played soccer, and my mom was amazed by it. Title IX didn't exist when she was growing up, so the concept of being a girl and being athletic was foreign to her. She had never even entertained the idea, because it just wasn't a possibility for her. We've come a long way, but in some respects we've also taken steps backward. We have more freedom in our educations, in our careers, in our reproductive rights, but there is this regression toward the "Lolita" phenomenon, which really bothers me. I grew up with Madonna and other female icons who were sexual, but they *owned* it. They were in control, and they had the brains to back it up. Today pop culture is full of images of young women who are very sexual and provocative, but they're not the ones in control of their image—they're just put out there by their handlers for public consumption. They project this powerful image, but it's not backed up by anything. They're not really expressing anything; they're using their ability to turn men on as a way of selling albums or movie tickets. It's not even so much a feminist issue for me, it's more of an artistic issue—it's an empty product.

Whenever I read a script or a play, I read the female character and try to imagine it written as a male character. There's nothing wrong with a female character's being sexual or being comfortable in her femininity or being sultry, but I want to make sure the character has the depth that is usually found in male characters. The paradigm for a female character can go all the way back to Dante—the image of a woman as the muse. The male character is inspired by her, but that gets old after a while. I want to know what she is thinking, what her problems are. That's something I can relate to. I think we're getting there. There is good material out there, and a lot of really talented actresses who you are seeing in more and more meaningful roles.

I think that women's issues are slightly more personal, because it's very easy to put myself in other women's shoes. When women are in their teens and twenties, it seems that they are sort of afraid of each other, which is unnatural, because girls have such a sense of community. But we need to talk more. If women's issues were talked about on a regular basis, they wouldn't fall by the wayside. It's easy to walk around wondering, *Am I strange because I'm uncomfortable with the way things are going? Am I strange because I had this experience? Are my feelings unique? Do other women feel this way?* We just have to open up, and inevitably we all realize that we are experiencing the same thing, but it is not talked about on a larger scale, unless we keep trying.

Julia Stiles

Judy Woodruff

CNN anchor Judy Woodruff is a founding cochair of the International Women's Media Foundation, an organization dedicated to promoting and encouraging women in the communications industries. Her 1982 book This Is Judy Woodruff at the White House *recounts her experiences as a journalist. Among her many awards, she was the first recipient of the National Women's Hall of Fame President's 21st Century Award. She serves on the board of advisers for the John S. Knight Journalism Fellowships at Stanford University and the Freedom Forum First Amendment Center and is on the board of directors for the Carnegie Corporation of New York and the Urban Institute. She is a graduate of Duke University.*

MY FAMILY MOVED to Augusta, Georgia, when I was about to enter the seventh grade, after two years in Taiwan. My father was in the army, and we were one of the few military families in our comfortable, middle-class neighborhood in this medium-size Southern city. It was the tail end of the 1950s, and my beloved mother, like most other women of the era, had stayed home to raise my sister and me.

I saw how dependent she was on my father for just about

everything: income, transportation (she couldn't drive), and social life. I quietly decided I wanted something different. In fact, my mother encouraged me to do what she had not done: go to college and pursue a career. I didn't know then *what* career. There were few role models. Most of the mothers of my friends also stayed home, but a few worked outside the home. One was the county treasurer, an exalted position back then for a woman; another was a nurse, and I remember she worked very long hours—many nights and weekends. Several were socially active, attending bridge parties and doing volunteer work. I particularly admired one for her free spirit and outspoken ways. I suspected that she drank during the day, but that never slowed her down; indeed, it made her more intriguing to me, as she held together a large, busy family!

But the women who, as a group, had the greatest influence on me were a handful of schoolteachers, most older and unmarried—what used to be called, unkindly, "spinsters." I know their names by heart, and a few are still alive: Naomi Williams, who taught me Shakespeare in eighth and ninth grades; Winnie Overstreet, who taught me French in tenth, eleventh, and twelfth grades; Marie Hulbert, who taught me biology in tenth and twelfth grades; and Jacqueline Marshall, who taught me English in the eleventh grade. They all were incredibly smart, incredibly self-confident, and extremely dedicated, and I was caught in their spell for much of the time I sat in their classrooms. I recited sonnets to Miss Williams, I dissected frogs for Miss Hulbert, who wore her gray hair pulled back severely in low knot, a style that never changed over the years I knew her. To be sure, I complained along with all the rest of my classmates about how hard they worked us. I recall feeling intimidated on many occasions. But I loved them, and I learned more and was shaped more by them, than by any other female figures of my early life, besides my mother.

There were also a couple of young female teachers, just out of college: Barbara Bowen, who taught eighth-grade math and was a bundle of energy and constant encouragement, and a drama teacher, who pushed me to act in the school plays. Later, after I reached college, a political-science professor, Carolyn Happer, truly opened my eyes to the wonders of politics and government, which became my major.

All these women made a difference, in contrast to some of my male teachers, like the one who taught me physics in the twelfth grade and felt that girls really had no business taking the course. He almost never called on me or the one other girl in his class, except to ridicule us. He and the college calculus professor, who treated his women students like we were idiots, turned me against math as a career. That was no great loss in my case, but I'm sad when I think of all the other potential female talent wasted because of their attitudes.

I often wondered where I got the nerve to look into a television camera and to write about and report the news, especially political news. For a long time, I didn't know the answer. I often said, when asked, that there were no female role models in my early life. But as I've grown older and thought back about these extraordinary women teachers,

I've realized it was they who helped make me who I am to-day. They set an example by dedicating themselves to their students. I was awfully lucky to have passed through the doors of their classes. I hope they know what they gave me and so many others.

Nina Totenberg

As the network's legal-affairs correspondent, Nina Totenberg has become an instantly recognizable voice to thousands of National Public Radio listeners for her Supreme Court reporting. During her award-winning career, she has covered important stories such as the Clarence Thomas–Anita Hill controversy, the papers of Supreme Court Justice Harry Blackmun, the Clinton impeachment inquiry, and the high court's Florida election ruling. She is also a regular panelist on the television program Inside Washington *and has published articles in a wide range of newspapers and magazines.*

MY FATHER'S VIEW was that I could do anything. He never said, "Oh, you can't do that." Never. As a concert violinist, he was in a profession where there were women at the top of the heap. Not a ton of them, but they were there. My mother, anxious that I not be alone, told me that I should not let boys know that I was smarter than they were. I told her I wasn't going to do that. If they weren't smart enough to keep up, I wasn't interested in them anyway. Probably not true. But I wanted it to be.

I never considered not having a career. Women who grew

up in the 1950s were not, by and large, supposed to have careers, nor were they supposed to be better than men in certain things. I wanted to be better than men in a *lot* of things, and I wanted to have a career and a husband. So for me it was torture. But I'm very pigheaded, and I just figured I could do it if anybody ever gave me the chance. Or I would *make* them give me a chance.

I wasn't a brilliant or dedicated student, but I was very good at writing and class discussions. As a young adult, I was told over and over that I couldn't do a particular kind of reporting, but each time I tried, I was able to do it perfectly well.

My first newspaper job was working at the *Record-American* in Boston, which doesn't exist anymore. There was only one regular woman reporter, a very good crime reporter. I worked on the women's page, which in those days was really boring—recipes and fashion, and I didn't get to do the fashion. I did the society page when the society editor went on vacation. I wrote the wedding announcements, which I considered a great step up.

I started going out at night with various reporters as their "legman." I would go out with the staff photographer, who had a Boston police, state police, and fire-department radio in the car. We would zoom around, chasing one crisis after another.

There just wasn't enough for me to do during the day, so I tried to find stories. In the mid-1960s, women couldn't get contraceptive devices without a prescription. To find out what the colleges were doing about this, I called around to the health-service departments at all the universities and colleges in the area, pretending to be a student, and made appointments to get contraceptives. I was twenty-one. I wrote it up as a proposal and brought it to the executive editor of the paper, a guy named Eddie Holland, a very nice man, who looked at me in absolute horror and said, "I cannot let you do this" (meaning have lots of physical exams). So I didn't, because he wouldn't let me. Eventually I did other things. That shows you what sorts of limits were imposed on a young woman even then. And it shows my willingness to accede to them, to some extent.

A few years later, when the presidential primaries were in New Hampshire and my newspaper wasn't particularly interested in my covering them, I went up at night, wrote the pieces, and I sold the work as a freelancer.

There were a couple of other women in the press corps. Marianne Means showed up every now and then, and a wonderful person, Nan Robertson, who subsequently won the Pulitzer Prize for the New York Times. I was not beloved on the press bus because I wasn't one of the boys. I wasn't included in much of anything. To this day, I don't quite understand how I was so determined to be part of a group that didn't want me, except of course, as the target of the occasional "pass."

One day, Nan walked onto the bus. She was very elegant, and she knew everybody. They all said, "Hi, Nan, hi, Nan," and I was sitting there by myself. She walked over and sat down next to me. I have never forgotten that. It's why I have always loved her. She befriended me when she was a very important reporter and I was nobody.

I remember thinking I was going to have to use being a woman to my advantage. I batted my eyelashes at stupid politicians and got them to tell me things. That's all I did, but it worked. When I was young and lovely and looked at them like I was a dumb blonde, they would say quite remarkable things. They weren't used to women reporters.

In those days, I would go the White House Correspondents Dinner and be one of a half dozen women out of a thousand or fifteen hundred guests. And I was the youngest by thirty years. I would always wear a low-cut dress and go to the parties afterward. People would get very drunk, and they would stare down my dress and blather their little heads off. On two or three occasions, I got really big scoops out of those dinners.

I think the fact that there are so many women reporters now has changed the nature of the business quite a bit. When I was first reporting in Washington, I would go out on the campaign trail, and it was considered totally acceptable that candidates for national political office were philandering their way though the airplane with their young staff aides. You couldn't do that now, largely because women are on the plane. There are also limits on the way we operate in terms of hours and what's expected of people relative to their jobs. Editors now understand that both women reporters and men reporters have children. Well, they sort of understand.

The advice I would give young women would be to pick your battles. Don't fight over everything. Figure out what is really important to you. Young women are accustomed to getting most of what they want these days, at least in the short run, because they don't hit the glass ceiling until they are in their thirties, forties, or fifties. Because of this, they often have big fights over insignficant things. In everyone's life there are important moments when you're going to have to fight for something. Just make sure you haven't used up all your capital over something that wasn't worth fighting over to begin with.

I can only speak from my personal experience, but another thing I'd say to a young person is that your life is going to be very different at different statges. I've never been divorced, for example, or been a single mother who had to take care of children by myself, but I've had friends who have had those experiences. When you're quite young, the thing that you have the most of is time. As a young reporter, I would put in unbelievable hours. I would wait till midnight or two o'clock in the morning to reach somebody at home on the West Coast, maybe someone who was dodging me.

Frankly, I wouldn't do that now. I have a life. But when I was in my twenties, that *was* my life. That was what I did. Two weekends ago, I was in the office at eight o'clock in the morning two days in a row because of a story I was pursuing. But those times are rare.

My weekends are mine, unless there's some very pressing reason for them not to be. I have a wonderful husband. I was married for twenty years, and my husband died. I have lost one husband, which is enough to teach you that you better value every moment you have when you have a good one. I've been lucky enough to find a second great one, and I'm not missing out on any moments that I can have with him. But that's the view of someone in her late fifties.

This is not so much a female thing as it used to be. I was very amused in the last presidential election when I went out to cover the vice presidential campaigns. The press corps that covers these campaigns is not big. I was on Air Force Two, and it's quite small, relatively speaking, so at the most there were ten or twelve reporters on board. Once we would get to our destination in the evening, I, as the foot-loose and fancy-free veteran, would say to anyone around, "Would you like to go get a drink?" No one did, because they all wanted to call home. They were all checking in with their spouses and children before bedtime, and most of them were men. They were all going to spend an hour on the phone instead of with me at the bar.

Times have changed—for the better.

Luisah Teish

Luisah Teish, born and raised in New Orleans, is a priestess of Oshun, the African Yoruba goddess of love. She is a performer, writer, and ritual designer. Her books include Jambalaya: The Natural Woman's Book of Personal Charms and Practical Rituals and Carnival of the Spirit: Seasonal Celebrations and Rites of Passage. She is a member of the faculty of the University of Creation Spirituality and a board member of the Association for Transpersonal Psychology.

I WAS SEVEN YEARS OLD when my mother announced that I was "not a baby anymore" and that she was no longer "responsible for my sins." She believed that she had fulfilled her obligation by having me christened in the African Methodist Episcopal Church in accord with the tradition of my father's clan.

Seven is a mystical age for Southern black people. Becoming seven meant that my spirit was now solidly placed in my body and my mind was secure. I received instructions in how to conduct myself socially and was given increased responsibility in the maintenance of the house. Turning seven also granted me the privilege of reading the newspaper. What a terrible world I found there!

Although I'd been christened in the church in deference to the rites of my father's family, my mother's policy had been "God by any means necessary." This meant that I could go to any accessible church irrespective of the denomination. Then an important change occurred. My mother informed me that I had to "become Catholic" in order to fulfill a deathbed promise she'd made to Papa, her father. So she enrolled me in a Catholic school in Algiers, Louisiana, two towns away, because this was the closest Catholic church that admitted black people. St. Rosalie, the local Catholic church, was segregated, and "the children of Cain" were forbidden to pass through its doors. I tried to attend St. Rosalie's once and got chased across the tracks by little white boys with big sticks and stones.

With each year, the confusion about God, racism, and my place in the world mounted. By the time I was nine, I had moved from "no longer being a child" into some netherworld with no identity at all. With the onset of menstruation at twelve, I was told that I was "a woman now," with no explanation for the changed expectations of the adults and no occasion to mark the change for my understanding.

My mother had always told me that I was smart and talented, that I could sing like a bird and dance like a centipede. She'd always encouraged my efforts and admonished me to be the best at whatever I did. This led me to believe that someday somebody would really love me. But by the time I reached fourteen, I'd also been bombarded with all the assaults mainstream American culture could dish out to a girl. There were requirements and taboos around my body, my mind, my space, and my relationships that made little or no sense to me.

At the same time, the library offered me other possibilities to consider. I read of black women who were powerful. There was Harriet Tubman, who liberated slaves from the plantations, and Mam'zelle Marie Laveau, the voodoo queen who created a spiritual culture in the bayous of New Orleans. Television reminded me of Rosa Parks, the civil-rights activist who crossed the white line to the front of the segregated bus and initiated a movement that affected an entire nation! I wanted to be like them. I tried to be like them.

Secretly I longed to be sexually daring like Eartha Kitt and Mae West, and I imagined that when I was sixteen I would be beautiful—in truth, at sixteen I was ugly and miserable.

By the time I was twenty, I became an "animist." I wrapped my body in the brilliant fabrics of a West African woman. Each head wrap had a meaning that addressed a woman's occupation and status in the community: midwife, market woman, queen mother.

I shaved my head bald in honor of my Masai sisters in East Africa. I pierced my nose, painted my face, and wore three earrings in my ears as a sign of my heritage as African royalty. Each of these acts was preceded by a period of study about the people and the culture they came from. And each adornment was received in the context of a ritual, based on my studies. Proudly I paraded down the street balancing fruit baskets on my head, as my Caribbean sisters do.

I found folklore that contained stories of African goddesses: Yemonja, the great mother of the ocean; Oya, the queen of the winds of Change; and Oshun, the goddess of love. These goddesses represented the collective stories of the lives of generations of women who walked the earth and functioned as "daughters of nature." And I loved it! It told me that it was natural to be powerful. It said that as a "daughter of the Goddess" I could, through initiation, become a "mother of the spirits." I could be powerful, as my ancestors had been. And I wanted to be. So I took a path that has led me to the place where I stand today. A place where I am priestess, teacher, and activist.

When I look in the mirror, I see a beautiful woman. My thick lips, coffee-colored skin, and salt-and-pepper hair reflect back to me a heritage of power and a life well lived. My brown eyes look deep into the mirror and see more than a reflection of myself.

I see my ancient African mothers, my Native American grandmothers, my Asian sisters, my Latin cousins, and my European friends. I see a long line of women standing behind me reflecting the past that I've inherited. They move backward in time until they become sheer femaleness, that primal energy that is present in all things, in animals, in plants, in the earth herself. When I look into the mirror, I see myself as a cell in the body of the Goddess. And I am proud to be a woman, and especially proud to be my own woman.

This reflection in the mirror allows me to start my day

with confidence, to overcome fear of failure, to combat the
negative messages that are thrown at me every day by the
media, by misogynist men, and by other women who hate
themselves through me. This reflection of the Goddess allows me to stand tall in the face of danger, to work steadily
toward my goals, and to support love and surrender to spirit.
Because of knowledge of the Goddess working in and
through me, I can withstand the vicissitudes of fate. When I
look in the mirror, I see thousands of beautiful women.

Luisah Teish

Lillian Vernon

Born in Leipzig, Germany, Lillian Vernon moved with her family to Holland and then America to escape the perils of World War II. She attended New York University and in 1951 started her well-known and extremely successful mail-order business, the Lillian Vernon Corporation. She serves on the boards of numerous nonprofit organizations, including the Kennedy Center, Lincoln Center, New York University's College of Arts and Science, and the Children's Museum of the Arts. She has received many awards, including the Ellis Island Medal of Honor, the Big Brothers Big Sisters National Hero Award, and the Direct Marketing Hall of Fame Award.

IN 1951, FEW WOMEN worked outside the home or owned their own businesses. In general, men and many women considered a businesswoman unfeminine and an intruder in a man's world. The cultural message I grew up with was to be content as a wife and mother, or possibly a secretary, teacher, or nurse. If a woman chose a career other than the stereotype, she usually worked with her husband, like my mother, who helped my father run his leather-goods business after my family fled Germany before the onset of World War II.

When I conceived the idea to start my mail-order business at home, it never occurred to me that I might be trespassing on male territory and stepping into a potentially hostile world. But I certainly didn't let prejudice or any preconceived ideas deter the dream I had. If I had not been endowed with the entrepreneurial spirit that my father helped nurture at an early age, I might never have had the courage to forge ahead. I needed money, and I figured out how to get it in a way that suited my particular circumstances at the time. I was a young, married housewife expecting my first son, and I never dreamed that my company would eventually become a leading national catalog and online retailer.

Looking back, I am reminded that anything is possible for women who follow their dream and passion.

Lillian Vernon

Tatum O'Neal

Born to actor Ryan O'Neal and actress Joanna Moore in 1963, Tatum Beatrice O'Neal won a Best Supporting Actress Academy Award for her performance in Peter Bogdanovich's Paper Moon *(1974). At age ten, she was the youngest actress ever to win an Oscar. With* The Bad News Bears *in 1976, Tatum became the highest-paid child star in film history. After filming* Nickelodeon, *she returned in* International Velvet *in 1978 and* Little Darlings *in 1980. In 1986, she married the tennis star John McEnroe, and this stormy marriage produced three children: Kevin, Sean, and Emily. The two divorced in 1994. Her recent films include* The Scoundrel's Wife *and* The Technical Writer. *Her autobiography,* A Paper Life, *was published in October 2004.*

WHEN I WAS LITTLE, I lived with my mother, Joanna Moore; her sixteen-year-old boyfriend; and some runaway boys. We lived on a ranch in California that had barely any running water.

My mother was strung out on speed, and her boyfriend was hitting us all the time. He was brutal. We had a big tree on the ranch, and he would take these roots and whip me with them. I tried to run away a bunch of times to get away from him—

I was very defiant. As a tiny little person, I was very righteous about what was right and wrong, and I knew I was being treated badly. I'd stand there with my arms folded and my chin up and say, "You can't hit my brother like that. You can't treat me like this."

I'd beg my mother to please save me, but she couldn't. My brother, Griffin, remembers her in this fur poncho, sitting in the ivy and telling him, "Do you see them? Do you see the people? Do you see them? They're here. They're here." He was only six at the time, but he was very mature and he'd say to me, "Do you see that Mom's, like, sitting in the ivy with a poncho covering her, looking out, looking like total insanity?" It *was* insanity. It was just day after day of insanity.

Griffin and I were starving. I was sleeping on a bathroom floor; I had scars on my legs; I had been totally brutalized. I had been molested, attacked, beaten up, and screamed at. I begged my dad to save me. I'd plead with him, "Please, please take me away from here. I hate it." One day, when I was about seven, he came in his fancy car to get me. But I didn't get to stay with him right away. Instead I was sent to a boarding school in Arizona for "dysfunctional kids." I hated it. Six months after my arrival, I cut off all my hair, put it in a package, and sent it to my grandmother. She was always coming in and saving my life. I put a note in the package—I wrote "I hate it here" a hundred times. Those were the few words I knew how to spell. I was like a little urchin from *Tobacco Road*. So they took me out of that terrible place, and I went to live with my father. I went to school, but the trauma I had undergone made me too different—I couldn't relate to people and I didn't fit in at all. I was such a weirdo and had this tough "my dad's a movie star" thing going. I pushed people away.

My dad said, "You have the opportunity to not go to school. Tatum, they're about to make this movie." And I was going to be in it—like I had any idea what that meant. A week before filming started, I broke my arm while playing at my friend's house. I cried, but my father didn't believe it was broken. Finally, three days later, he took me to the doctor. We went to Kansas to film the movie. I had a broken arm for the first few weeks, but they hid it underneath clothes. It was hard shooting the movie, and I was kind of lonely, but it was good fun for me being a kid in the midst of things. When we did the carnival scene, I went on that ride like fifty times and ended up getting sick.

Things with my dad were pretty good until I won an Academy Award. He didn't even come with me that night—my grandparents took me. He was really loving to me until I got more attention than he did. Then he hated me. Literally hated me. Forever.

Imagine, I had the most beautiful women in the world around me all the time. Ursula Andress, Bianca Jagger, Anjelica Huston—all these exotic, world-famously beautiful women were in my life, not caring for me, but they were always there. I tried to become like them, but the thing is, I don't know what it's like to be a girl. They had so many fine clothes, and I'd think, *If I had that silk shirt or I was prettier, maybe he would like me.* I remember suffering, crying outside his door. Just take me, help me, save me. But he always picked whomever he was with over me.

He used to make me play Farrah at racquetball, and he hit me whenever I was late. She was so skinny, and I had gotten heavy. My dad tried to get me to use coke to lose weight— he was doing it. I was fifteen, really awkward, with frizzy hair, and there Farrah was, at the height of her career, and he'd make me play her at her house. I'd have to walk down the hallway with all of her magazine covers, and she'd be playing racquetball in her little shorts with her hair flying, and he's above us yelling to me, "Get your racquet back! Get your racquet back! Get in front of her!"

I'm not going to get into the psychology of it, but I'm glad I got away, because I would have died. Or I would have disfigured my face with a million face lifts like some of the other women in his life. But I didn't, because I say you either love me or you don't. I feel as women it's our responsibility to get away from men like that. I didn't choose my father, but I chose to leave home.

For years, I was adamant about pushing people away, because I didn't trust anybody. I would look at people and I wouldn't smile, wouldn't give them the time of day. I was working on getting clean and recovering, and I didn't care if people thought I was a bitch. I was so mad that I didn't particularly love life, and I just wanted people to stay away from me.

But at thirty-nine years old, I had some kind of really weird epiphany, a rude awakening or something. And I thought, *Hey, it kind of works better when you're your genuine self. When you let people see how nice you are. That you're not going to be afraid. No one's going to hurt you. No one will steal your heart away and tear it up and throw it at you. You're going to be okay.*

In the past, I have not been embraced by the women of the Hollywood community. I think now I am. As I'm entering my forties, people are really starting to be proud of me. People are really happy to see me. This is good. I want to be a role model for younger women and women my age and women who are older. My own role models have not been that good, besides Meryl Streep and Sissy Spacek. I did so much soul-searching in therapy, just trying to figure out who I am.

You know what I've learned throughout all of this? What I would say to my daughter or any girl? I would say to believe in yourself, love yourself, and speak through your feelings. Don't be afraid to be heard.

Beverly Sills

Born in Brooklyn, New York, Sills spent the first ten years of her life in its Crown Heights neighborhood. Her professional career began at the age of three, when she appeared as Bubbles Silverman on Uncle Bob's Rainbow House *radio show. She began touring as an opera singer at the age of fifteen. A renowned member of the New York City Opera from 1955 to 1980, she performed in the world's greatest opera houses, recorded eighteen full-length operas and numerous solo collections, and appeared in hundreds of television programs. She is the author of an autobiography entitled* Bubbles: A Self-Portrait. *Sills served as general director and then president of the New York City Opera, and in 1993 she became the first woman, the first performing artist, and the first former head of an arts company to be named chair of the Lincoln Center for the Performing Arts. She has served on numerous boards and was the national chair of the March of Dimes Mothers' March on Birth Defects.*

I WAS RAISED IN a European household, so it was very puritanical, with lots of sentences with huge periods at the end of them. When I was seven, my father called me into the living room, so I knew it was a special occasion. The furniture was covered with sheets so it wouldn't fade. I really never did find out what color that furniture was. He said to me, "Your mother doesn't drink and your mother doesn't smoke, and neither will you."

So I never did.

He also told me that only my two brothers would go to college and that I had to be married by my seventeenth birthday—my mother and I never figured out why seventeen, and not eighteen or nineteen. He then said, "If you are not married by then, the only respectable profession is teaching school." How I was supposed to do this without a college education was simply not discussed. I then told him I wanted to be a famous opera star. My father said, "Nice girls do not go on the stage. Only hussies go on the stage." I asked him what a hussy was. He said, "It's somebody who wears low-cut dresses, changes the color of her hair, and wears too much makeup."

I was hooked.

Beverly Sills

Vanessa Williams

Born March 18, 1963, in Westchester County, New York, singer/actress Vanessa Lynn Williams has received fourteen Grammy nominations and was the first African-American to hold the title of Miss America. On Broadway, she starred in Kiss of the Spider Woman *and the Kennedy Center production of* Carmen Jones. *Her film credits include* Eraser *(1996),* Dance with Me *(1998),* Shaft *(2000), and* Johnson Family Vacation *(2004).*

"Darling" is the word that comes to mind when I think about growing up female. When you're a child, you're perceived as a little darling. When you're a wife, "darling" is a term of endearment, and when you achieve things, it's darling to achieve whatever good fortune comes your way. It connotes sweetness and femininity, but it also has a lot to do with good luck and accomplishment.

I was fortunate enough to have a really good foundation from my parents, from the environment that I was given. My mother is a survivor, a fighter, and a leader, and my dad is a nurturer, a true teacher with the patience of Job. It was a great combination to grow up with. They were both educators, and their lives were parenting and early childhood development. Those years were the strongest and most formative years for me, and I try to implement a lot of what they gave me with my own kids.

My parents treated my brother and me alike. I was never pampered or coddled or isolated from doing chores. I mowed the lawn. I had to do my Saturday-afternoon chores, which were cleaning the bathrooms and the toilets. I was not treated like a princess with special privileges. We were both treated equally. If we behaved and lived by the rules, we got a chance to do things. If we didn't, we were grounded. When we were kids, there was a sense of freedom and adventure. We'd go into the woods to explore, ride our bikes to the deli to get a sandwich, knowing we'd ridden a mile by ourselves. These were the little tests we were allowed to do because it was a safe environment.

I remember a traumatic incident when I was in the fourth grade. I was riding my beat-up, heavy metal bike down a steep hill with my cousin on the back—a stupid thing to do. Neither of us was wearing a helmet. The gravel was slippery; we rounded a corner too fast, and we wiped out. The handlebar went into my thigh, and as I slid down the street on my face, I chipped my front tooth. My mother heard my scream and came running over. All I remember was her saying, "Oh, Vanessa, your face. What were you thinking?" I just wanted to be taken care of, but now that I am a mother, I know I'd be every bit as mad at my kids for doing the same thing. When you're a parent, your fear goes directly into anger. I remember crying in bed, thinking,

Why did I do this to myself? My face is a mess. Will I ever look the same? That was my self-inflicted wound, my first giant stupid moment.

Growing up, I often felt like an outsider. My school was an entirely white environment, so I always viewed myself as different. My hair texture was different, my skin color was different. I was praised for my talent rather than my looks. I was the one that people would see on the stage and say, "That girl's going to Broadway. Watch out for that girl, you'll see her name up in lights," not "Oh, she's a great beauty." But I loved it. I'd much rather have people come up and say they respect me or they love my work or that a song moved them than, "Oh, you're a lot prettier in person than you are on TV." How do you respond to that?

I never set out to be a beauty queen. During my sophomore year at Syracuse University, I was majoring in musical theatre and appearing in a lot of shows. The local Miss Greater Syracuse pageant people scouted their talent at the college. One of their representatives came to my show and asked if I would do the pageant. At first I said no. But I needed scholarship money, so I called my mom to see what she thought. She told me to go ahead and try to get the scholarship money. Six months later, I was Miss America. Again I had the feeling of being an outsider and just observing. For many of those women, the pageant was their whole life; all their hopes and dreams revolved around it. From the time they were young, they were Little Miss this and that. But for me, at twenty years old, it was my first time in the Miss America system.

I was a phenomenon because I was the first black Miss America. Besides the normal Miss America circuit I was expected to do, black organizations that had never cared about the pageant suddenly wanted me to appear at their functions. The media loved having a controversy that went against the standard. And I was an outspoken, pro-ERA, pro-choice twenty-year-old from New York who wasn't afraid to state her opinions. Particularly in the South, since I'm a Northern Yankee, having a black Miss America created a lot of hostility—it wasn't long before I got my first round of hate mail. There were threats against my parents and my family. I made an appearance in Alabama and had to have an armed guard outside my motel door. I did a parade down there and had to stay in the car because of sniper threats. It was scary, and by November I was exhausted and started thinking, *When is this going to be over?* This was before *the photos.*

I was tipped off by a *New York Post* reporter when I was up at the New York State pageant. He asked me something about Geraldine Ferraro, and then he said, "Oh, by the way, we heard that you're appearing in *Penthouse* magazine next month, September issue." I asked him what he was talking about. He said he'd heard it from very reliable sources. After my lawyer got involved, I told my parents. I told them that *Penthouse* was going to publish a magazine spread of some photos that had been taken of me, and I was so sorry. They said, "We forgive you," and that's all I needed to hear. I felt emotionally grounded. It was what I needed to persevere.

From that time until it all hit the fan, it was like an out-of-body experience. Watching images of yourself on television. Dan Rather, Jane Pauley, and Bryant Gumbel talking about you. People were commenting on the Miss America image and the image in the photos, and I was the person in between—a normal twenty-one-year-old who had done things in her past. Unfortunately, the one time I did, it was on film, and that doesn't happen to many people.

The first phase of it was the terror and the fright about what people were going to say and what was going to happen. Then the Miss America people decided to take the crown away. It was Al Marks, the head of the pageant at the time, who was demanding the crown back. My parents and other people said I should fight it. I just said, "Let me resign and move on with my life." I had only six weeks of the year left anyway. I had met the president, sung with Bob Hope, traveled the country, done the gig. If I wasn't being supported by the organization for which I felt I had done a great job over the past ten, eleven months, why fight?

People ask me if I could do it all over again, what would I do? I wouldn't be Miss America. Even though it was fantastic, my real joy in life is to be onstage. Had I graduated from Syracuse and gone to Yale, which is where I wanted to go for graduate work, then come to New York, I'm sure I would have been in the same place I am now in terms of my career. But, obviously, those aren't the cards that were dealt for me, and what I went through was meant to be.

Now my image is, I think, the working mother who does

it all—Broadway and television and film and recording—and who has four kids. That's my image now. My family, my kids, are my anchor.

I advise my daughters to enjoy life, not to grow up too fast. I always wanted to seize life and be older, but you need to enjoy the time and freedom you have when your parents are taking care of you. The safety net won't be there forever. I also tell them to honor their inner voice. Putting on a mask, pretending to be happy or trying to be somebody they aren't, is never necessary. Always know that when their gut feels that something is not good, then it's not good. Don't try to please. Don't try to be nice. Be strong enough to voice their opinion or voice their thoughts, because they'll be much happier in the end.

Suze Orman

*Achieving and maintaining financial security ranks as one of peoples'
major sources of anxiety today. Few understand this better than Suze
Orman, an internationally acclaimed personal finance expert,* New
York Times *bestselling author, and Emmy Award–winning talk-
show host whom* USA Today *called a "one-woman financial advice
powerhouse" and "a force in the world of personal finance."*

*From her earliest childhood years and the stresses of her father
losing his business, to her post-college waitressing job, to her climb up
through the ranks of the investment world, Suze has been able to
translate her own experiences into frank, savvy financial advice that
has transformed the lives of millions of people around the world.*

AS A LITTLE GIRL, I never quite got why my mother would
stay with my father. She always seemed miserable. I wasn't clear
about what it was, but I could see it in her face.

They would fight, and my mother would run around the
house shutting the windows so that the neighbors couldn't
hear. She cared more about what other people thought of us
than about addressing whatever was happening.

I never understood why we couldn't just leave. I would say,

"Let's run away together, we can do this alone," and she would just look at me with these empty eyes. It wasn't that I didn't love my father, but I am not sure that I liked him very much when I was growing up. I did not understand why he did certain things and to this day I never will.

By the time I was about seven years of age, I already knew that I would not have to deal with the kind of problems that we had in our house, for you see I had conjured up a plan. I knew when the time was right I would simply commit suicide; therefore, life did not matter, none of this would matter. I didn't have to do well in school. I didn't have to do anything.

As I started to get older, I found myself reaching for love and attention from my friends in any way I could. Stealing money from my father's pockets to buy things for my friends, making up stories of bad things that happened to me so my friends would feel sorry for me—anything to get them to like me and give me the attention I couldn't get at home because my mother and father were so busy dealing with their own serious problems.

For instance, when I was in the sixth or seventh grade, we were all at my friend Leslie's, riding our bikes. I lived about half a mile from her, and we all left when it started to get dark. I purposely took a long time to get home. When I got there, I made up a story that somebody had tried to kidnap me but that I got away by hiding in an alley. My friends were called, the police were called, and all of it was a lie. I'm sure the police knew it was a lie because it didn't make sense. I wasn't smart enough to get away with a lie. Nobody's ever smart enough to get away with a lie. But I can distinctly remember that I just wanted attention.

My dad and I, as I have said, did not have the best of relationships, but as I look back I can say that he taught me a work ethic that is still with me today. Even when he was on his deathbed, he'd get up and go to work, because he needed to make money. Nothing could keep him down, and I learned that if he could do what he had to do given the health he was in, then I could do anything. But my mom's actions taught me an equally valuable lesson.

The ritual each day was to wait for my mom—her secretarial job was across town—to come to my dad's store after work so we could all go home together. One particularly snowy Chicago night, Dad was really struggling with his emphysema, and I was growing increasingly annoyed with my mother who was an hour and a half late to meet us. When she finally arrived, she explained that she had been about to get on the train when she noticed an elderly woman who was confused and did not know how to get home. So my mom had taken the woman home first and then she came to us.

I didn't really care about that older woman, and in my rebellious state I started to yell at my mom. My dad stopped me and said: "Suze, don't you ever yell at your mother again. You should have half the heart that she has. What this world needs is more people like your mother who really care about helping others, even if those others are strangers. Your problem, Suze, is you are so busy feeling sorry for yourself that you cannot even see your own greatness. You cause problems rather than solve them." This was a "lightbulb" moment for me, for I knew he was right.

I hope people understand that in their lives everything really does happen for the best. I now believe that when serious things happen, it's simply because you are strong enough to handle them. You have got to understand that you're never given more than you can handle. I believe that, I believe that, I believe that. Those who have a tremendous number of negative events in their lives are those who can handle them, and those events shape those people in great ways for years to come.

Here is the bottom line: You can't use the events of your life to hide behind. You just can't, because what you're really doing is hiding from yourself. Sometimes you simply have to be a warrior and not turn your back on the battlefield. You just have to go for it, no matter what.

I look at my life now and ask myself, "Would I change anything that has ever happened to me?" The answer is an emphatic no, not one thing, because everything that happened has made me the person I am today. I refuse to look back at those things that happened as an excuse for why I couldn't be what I want to be. Instead, they compelled me to be honest, compelled me to know that anything is possible, compelled me to become myself. And when you know who you are, then you have what it takes to reach your greatest potential.

Ruth Knafo Setton

Ruth Knafo Setton is the writer-in-residence at the Berman Center for Jewish Studies at Lehigh University and author of the novel The Road to Fez. *She has received fellowships from the NEA, PEN, the Sewanee Writers' Conference, the Wesleyan Writers' Conference, the Pennsylvania Council on the Arts, and Yaddo. Her writing has appeared in many anthologies and journals, including* Best Contemporary Jewish Writing, Wrestling with Zion, *and* National American Review.

AT NIGHT I READ BY FLASHLIGHT, squandered my sight. Blue motes of dust sneezed from broken pages, cracked bindings. This much was clear: Being a woman was a mysterious thing. I was thirteen, desperate for knowledge, avidly turning the yellowed pages of books I bought for dimes and nickels at used-book fairs. I adventured with Stevenson, Hitchens, and Sterne across deserts and through the human heart; their women were cameos of beauty, more powerful as ideals than characters. I waded through French and Russian novels, only to discover that Swann preferred the smell of a madeleine to that of a woman, musketeers and knights did very well without females, and adulterous wives threw themselves beneath trains.

I tried to ignore my aunt's raucous laugh as she informed me, "Women smell! Down there! You must wash and scrub every day. Twice a day! Wash and scrub, and don't stop until you're clean!" I blocked my ears to the class bully, Barbara Jones, who mocked the girls who hadn't gotten their periods yet (including me): "Just wait, suckers! You're gonna bleed down there and drip on everything and stink like pigs, and then guys are gonna poke you with their things, and you'll have babies and bleed till you die. Every girl in the world!"

No way. I wasn't going to leap onto train tracks or bleed for the rest of my life. I was born in Morocco—surely this curse hadn't crossed the seas. My mother would have warned me, wouldn't she? She had whispered that women were unclean in the eyes of rabbis. But what did old rabbis know? They weren't in the bathroom with me when I washed. When I got out of the shower, I sniffed deeply. I was clean, radiantly clean.

When Miss Miller, the seventh-grade English teacher, gave the assignment to write a creative story, my imagination soared. It was the first time in my life I'd been *asked* to write something creative. However, I had to remind myself: This was Miss Miller of the dreaded squat body, tadpole eyes, and lipless mouth, the school's self-appointed "guardian of morality." Despite fringes swaying from every part of her— wispy gray bangs, suede cowboy jacket, roped tassels dangling from the hem of her rough carpet skirt, Indian moccasins— she still appeared immovable, ancient, and rooted as a petri- fied tree. Worst of all were her huge red paws banging a long wooden ruler as she enforced the laws of her kingdom. "Kill the passive voice!" she shrieked. "Kill the passive parasites! Murder them stillborn! Before they infect other words!"

Miss Miller wanted something creative?

I'd be a fool to trust her—wouldn't I? Yet I needed to trust. If I didn't, I'd burst. My own beast skin—Donkeyskin's ash-strewn face—would drop to the ground, revealing the secret me in all her fierce power.

I wrote feverishly, borrowing heavily from the French author Colette, and called the story "The Smell of Love." The opening image: a large bed under an open window. The gold satin cover ripples and shimmers like a swirling sea. In the bed a man and woman scream at each other. He accuses her of cheating on him. She gets out of bed and throws a vase at him. He storms out, slamming the door behind him. She kicks the door and the wall, then climbs onto the bed to look out the window. He walks away without looking back. She sinks back into the bed as she realizes that he is truly gone. She sniffs his pillow, the sheets, breathes in the scent of their love. She gets up and sees his jacket hanging on the chair. Crying, she wraps it tightly around herself. After a while, she goes back to bed, kneels, and looks out the window. The sun is high in the sky. She holds out her arms in pleading. In the distance, a dark figure emerges into focus. As he moves closer, she recognizes him and cries out in joy. He looks up and smiles. The End.

I handed in my masterpiece, painstakingly typed on lined yellow paper, and dreamed of the glory that would be mine. Miss Miller would be stunned by the power and beauty of my story: "Why, Ruth, I never imagined you were so talented. I am proud to have you in my class."

A week later, she handed back the stories. All the others received theirs, grumbled and snickered as they checked their grades. Everyone but me.

"One person wrote an obscene story that played wild and fast with morality," said Miss Miller, voice quavering with emotion. "Filth about body odors and immoral intercourse. This person must learn the rules of life. This person will receive an F. This person's parents will be notified. I will show you what we do with filthy stories. We destroy them stillborn!"

Her thick red fingers shredded, sliced, diced the yellow sheets and threw the tiny scraps into the garbage can. The only copy! A hard black wind blew through the room, cut at my flesh. I couldn't turn my head, couldn't shut my eyes. I was filthy and lewd, dust motes exploding from my spine. I'd never be able to lift myself from this seat, never walk out of this classroom, never move beyond this moment.

I look back at that girl—huddled and panting in her beast coat, fighting the howl that was rising, even then, from deep within—and wish I could tell her that yes, her story was ripped to pieces, but long after she left and Miss Miller locked the door, the smell of women seeped inside and filled the dingy classroom. Spicy, smoldering, sultry. The smell of love. Unclean, unfathomable, unextinguished, unfinished. Open the door, girl: The story isn't over yet.

Esta Soler

In 1980, Esta Soler founded the Family Violence Prevention Fund. Working with private and government agencies, she established programs to protect women and children from all forms of abuse, and she has received many awards, including the Koret Israel Prize, a Kellogg Foundation National Leadership Fellowship, and the University of California Public Health Heroes Award. In 2002, the fund was chosen by Worth *magazine as one of America's 100 Best Charities.*

WHEN SHE WAS LITTLE, my daughter was reading a book and came across the word "matriarch." She said, "Mom, what is a matri-ache?" I corrected her pronunciation and described to her somebody who is very present in the home, who provides a clear sense of guidance, but somebody who is also very warm and nurturing. I was waiting for her to say, "Oh, somebody like Grandma," and then it dawned on me that she didn't know Grandma.

For me, my daughter's asking me what a matriarch was brought back memories of the way in which I grew up in a home with a mom who was all of those things. I always saw a tremendous amount of learning and strength in her. When my mother was eighteen, she went to New York to try to get passports for some of my relatives to come to the United States so they would survive the Holocaust. If the community needed someone to sit at a table and figure out what to do, they called my mother.

In my household, there was a kind of role reversal. My mother was the strong one who always took charge; my dad was the one who cried, the one all the kids in the neighborhood wanted to play with. Because my mother was so strong, it was sometimes hard to meet her expectations.

Mine was an interesting family. When I was young, we lived in a small apartment in Bridgeport, Connecticut, with my two aunts, Margie and Harriet, plus my mom and dad. My Auntie Margie, whom my daughter is named after, got married when I was five and moved out. I continued to share a bedroom with my Aunt Harriet.

Aunt Margie and Uncle Ernie had three children, Sarah, Marcie, and Molly. They ultimately wound up living within a block of us, so we basically all lived together. Margie died of breast cancer, and my cousins grew up with their father. Because their mother died young, my mother became the central mother figure in their lives. So in reality, even though I'm an only child, I never felt like one. My mother was very clear about that, about how we were one big family. Now we all have children, and all the kids treat each other like first cousins.

Bridgeport, Connecticut, was a very working-class city. I didn't realize it then, but I went to a pretty tough elementary school. One day, I came home from school and said that

I had been called a kike. I didn't even know what that was, but I was mad about it. My mother said to me, "We're going to take care of this." The next day, she went to school and demanded that the principal do something about it, demanded that the teachers know something about anti-Semitism. That's where I got my political training. I didn't get it through reading, I got it through watching my mother. I thought, *Wow, I can have an effect on my life. I don't have to just take what happens to me.*

What I feel most is the comfort she provided for us. In my house, you were met with love and open arms. I think that everybody should have that. It's always been my mission to spread that feeling as much as I possibly can. I don't want to be a Pollyanna about it. You can't just will it, you have to work very hard to achieve it. I'm sure my parents suffered in ways that I wasn't even aware of. There was no money. Times were often hard. Yet they were able to communicate what was most important. What was most important to them was that there was food on the table, the kids were healthy, and everybody could sit down and break bread together.

It was required that we be home for Shabbat on Friday night—you couldn't do anything else, you had to be there. We were like a mini community center; the table would be filled with people and laughter. It was a mixture of strength, kindness, and continuity. Sitting around that table, you got to know people over a long period of time. You knew their parents and their kids and their kids' kids. You felt connected. There's a connection we had that I'm still searching for. For me, it's not so much growing up female as it was growing up in a time when there were strong community connections. That really influenced the work that I do now.

Years later, when I felt the need to go home, I wouldn't tell my parents I was coming. I would surprise them, showing up on a Friday night because I knew they would be there. It was a constant, an anchor. When I feel like I'm losing my center, I go back to the feeling in my childhood home, with all the flavors of the Shabbat dinner and the people sitting around the table talking.

Life is just filled with inconsistencies. After I graduated from college and learned to be a leader, I left school. I got married right away. I married a wonderful man who went to Yale and then Yale Law School. Somewhere along the way, I decided I wasn't as smart as he was and became less assertive. I don't know why this happened. Marriage can be such a comfortable place. It certainly was for my generation, so easy to fall into. Let *him* figure out how to get where we're going. Let *him* figure out how we're going to make a living.

I remember having this dream where my husband wanted to write a book, and I thought about how great it would be to be in the audience when he went on the talk shows. It took me a long time to realize that *I* could do that. *I* could write the book. It took me ten years to rediscover my leadership skills and find my own intelligence again. I had a lot to learn from him. I didn't really feel that the reverse was true until later in the relationship—I think it's a common experience for women of our generation.

Finally Mark and I separated, and it was at that point I created the Family Violence Prevention Fund and took off on my own career. I want to write public policy and move people in the United States and internationally to reduce the level of violence. To get to a place of respect and love. There can be no greater gift to me than to have this job and to be able to do that—my upbringing was my training.

Esta Soler

Sylvia Boorstein

Sylvia Boorstein is one of the cofounders of the Spirit Rock Meditation Center in Woodacre, California, and is a senior teacher at the Insight Meditation Society in Barre, Massachusetts. Her books include Don't Just Do Something, Sit There; It's Easier Than You Think; The Buddhist Way to Happiness; *and* That's Funny, You Don't Look Buddhist.

MY GRANDMOTHER'S CORSELET was rosy pink, and she put it on her naked body as one puts on a lifejacket, arms through the armholes first, followed by wrapping and clasping and snapping and zipping. It covered her, shoulders to thigh. I watched her, mornings, from the vantage point of her bed in the room next to mine. Even now, as I picture her arranging big breasts in the bra cups, buckling them in on either side, and then hook-and-eyeing innumerable hooks and eyes down one whole side to hold the entire garment in place, I realize I am still seeing with five-year-old eyes. She was, as my mother was—as I am—a short person. In my memory, though, she is big. And my memory of the last step of the corselet procedure, the zipping up of a long zippered panel over the full length of the hooks and eyes to smooth the garment, makes me sit up a bit straighter.

My grandmother's best dress, the one she often wore to the monthly meetings of the First Przemyślany Women's Auxiliary, had two parts. The underneath part was a satiny black sheath with a round neck and short sleeves. Over that went a front-buttoning, see-through black coatdress with tiny flowers printed onto the chiffonlike fabric. She called it "my redingote dress," and until I looked up "redingote" in my dictionary to write this essay, I imagined it to be a Yiddish word. A redingote is "a dress or lightweight coat, usually belted, open along the entire front to reveal a dress or petticoat worn underneath it. Also, a man's long double-breasted overcoat, 'riding-coat,' 18th century."

My mother had two closets in her bedroom. One was lined with cedar that smelled good to me when she opened it to take out something woolen. The other closet, the "regular" one, was the one she stood in front of every morning as she dressed. She, unlike all the other mothers on our 1940s Brooklyn street, had a job—she was a typist in the Coney Island Hospital—and she dressed to go to work every morning. I sat on her bed too and watched her. She called her bra a brassiere, and I recall noting that she was able to hook it behind her without looking. Her girdle was rubbery, and after she stepped into it and pulled it up over her hips, she sat down to pull on silk stockings. The girdle had garters that hooked over the tops of the stockings to hold them up, and after my mother stood up again, she would look behind her legs to see that the stocking seams were straight. The seams on most of her stockings matched the color of the stockings, but some of them had dark, contrasting seams.

My mother had great shoes. They had high heels and open toes and ankle straps and bows attached in front. My favorite was a pair of green, ankle-strap platform shoes with bronze nailhead studs all around the platform. My friend Rosemary Leonardi and I played dress-up with my mother's clothes. We took turns wearing the red velour dressing gown and teetering around in the green platform shoes. We sprayed ourselves with perfume from the crystal atomizer on my mother's dressing table, and we put on as many of my mother's multiple necklaces and bracelets as we could manage. "Now I am the queen," one of us would say, and "I am the lady-in-waiting," the other would declare.

When I was thirteen, I had fantasies about wearing beautiful clothes. I wanted to be glamorous. I used pastels to color the fashion advertisements in the *New York Herald Tribune*. Once, when my mother stopped to admire the colors I'd chosen for a collection of very wide-brim spring hats, I said, "I feel bad that I'll never be able to wear hats like these. Short women can't wear big hats."

"Yes they can," my mother said. "You can wear anything you want. You just walk into a room with whatever hat you like on your head and look like you think it belongs there. Then everyone will say, 'What a great idea! Big hats on small women!' *You* decide the style."

I agree—in clothes and in life.

Helen Hunt

Helen Elizabeth Hunt was born June 15, 1963, in Culver City, California. The daughter of a director and a photographer, she developed an early love for acting. During the '70s and '80s, she appeared in a number of made-for-TV movies. In the '90s, she became the highest-paid TV actress in history for her multiple Emmy-winning role as Jamie Buchman in the hit NBC sitcom Mad About You. *In 1996 she starred in the blockbuster film* Twister, *and in 1998 she won an Academy Award for her performance in* As Good as It Gets, *making her the first actress to win both an Emmy and an Academy Award in the same year. In 2000 she starred in* Dr. T and the Women, Cast Away, Pay It Forward, *and* What Women Want.

"DELICATE" IS THE WORD I would choose to describe growing up female, but I would have to qualify it with an explanation. Another way to say it is "sensitive"—not necessarily in the psychological sense, but rather in the way litmus paper is sensitive to what is impressed upon it. For me, part of growing up female was being very sensitive to the dark and the light that I was around.

I think I am still to this day, maybe to a fault, deeply moved and changed by a kind word. And particularly and deeply moved by a harsh one. Throughout my life, this has enabled me to receive whatever people wanted to say or whatever help they wanted to give or whatever guidance they wanted to provide. There was a woman in my life, Judith, who took care of me when my parents were away. There was a slowed-down, in-the-earth, 100 percent honest quality that she brought to every exchange we have ever had, whether I was nine years old or forty. Not only was it kind and helpful, it became part of my compass. She spoke in a deeper voice and listened with bigger ears. When I would ask her very delicate questions, I felt I was getting back the absolute truth in such a simple, kind, and loving way. It made a very deep impression on me.

My sensitivity isn't a choice. It's like, I'm a Gemini, my eyes are hazel, and I'm sensitive. I was born in June, I'm five foot seven and a half, and I'm sensitive. There's no choice; it feels more like my nature. As I get older, I've been slightly less clumsy in managing a way to bring that sensitivity into the world. I know that as sensitive as I am, there's probably a protective shell around it that's equal to the sensitivity. That is why acting and writing are such good medicine for me. They create a circle, a container, a protective sort of ring around the sensitivity, so the sensitivity can have its day. The sensitive part of me can stretch and roll around and make art. When someone can write something true and complicated and deep for me to work with, whether the result is something silly and funny or stark and low down, that's the channel for the sensitive part of me to break through.

Part of being female is a deep desire not to have to be so careful. To be messier and to be chaotic and wet and wild. We're living in a time where we have to manage all the complicated parts of ourselves so we can get through the day. But more and more women are imagining a way of being, and living it too, where what it means to be a woman can run a little freer than it does in the Western world. My stepson is a painter—Jackson Pollock–like paintings. We have an art room, and on each wall is a huge wet, wild expression of who he is. If the colors were a little warmer, that might be what it looks like to be a woman.

There have been certain times in my life when I've had that completely freeing feeling of being a woman. I have an aunt who's my age, and when we were younger, we spent our time playing in the pool and hiding in back rooms of places where her parents worked. We spent hours dressing up and painting our faces. That was a time when we were just girls.

Recently I saw little girls embracing this exact feeling. One of my best friends has a daughter, and I'm her godmother. My goddaughter was having a sleepover, and we brought our new baby over to meet the girls. They had just painted their faces with face paint, and it was partially wiped off—their eyes were rimmed and red, they had green under their chins, and they were dressed in little nightgowns. It was like stepping into *A Midsummer Night's Dream*. They were really not from this place. They were like sprites running around our daughter asking questions: "Why does she suck like that?" "Why are we washing our hands?" "Why is her name MaKena Lei?" "I want her feet," one would say. "I want her toes," another would say. "I want all of her." We thought, This *is female; this isn't boys.* Boys are fun but this is something different—something very particular to being female. There was something feral and wild and untamed about those girls. And that just seemed exquisite and precious and uniquely female. Much more so than "delicate." It can only really be seen in the underworld . . . late at night when you come visiting with a new baby, or in the woods when you're face-painting with your little friend, or when you sexually come to life. It's a uniquely female version of feral, that is filled with energy and libido. I want that for my daughter. To be able to be feral like that. It's rare that any of us gets to see it or live it for a minute, but I believe it lives inside every woman.

Of course, a different kind of female power is experienced by giving birth. Twice I was in a room with a girlfriend of mine when she gave birth. Then, when I gave birth myself, I felt that there was something capital-*F* Female and capital-*P* Powerful going through me. It was powerful to be a vessel for whatever was making that happen. Some combination of my daughter and my wish and something bigger came together, and out came this human being.

When I was getting ready, leading up to having this baby, as much as you hear horror stories about the pains of labor and contractions, I was less afraid about that part and more afraid about actually pushing her out. I thought the contractions were going to be some muscular pain that I'd either be able to handle or not, but I had no fright about them. I had real fright about the pushing, partly because I imagined some flesh-tearing version of pain and also because it seemed like such an out-of-control thing to do. On the other side of the pushing was going to be something that, although it had been my deepest wish for the longest time, was unknown and beyond my control. Once I pushed her out, I couldn't keep tabs on her in the same way. While she was in there, I knew she was okay. But I knew as soon as she came out, I was just at the mercy of faith.

It turned out to be the opposite. The contractions were really hard to handle. But once I got into pushing, it wasn't painful at all, and I thought I could do it forever. I pushed for two hours. I feel like I could have pushed for twenty more. At first, I was pushing but I was also afraid. Like driving with the brake on, which probably explains why I wasn't making a lot of progress. Her father had said to me from the time I was about four or five months pregnant, "I feel like I know her already." I said, "Well, really I don't." I felt more like an animal whose job it was to get this creature out safe, and that was it. After about forty-five minutes of pushing, I kept hearing the doctor and the midwife and my boyfriend saying, "Yeah, good, good." They didn't sound like they really meant it. I closed my eyes and thought, *Okay, what do I need to be able to do this, to be able to really commit to doing this?* The one thing I thought of was that I could hold her, which had been my wish for so long. I started talking to her: "If you come out, we get to do this really good thing—I get to hold you." And the next time I pushed, I heard this swell of volume from everybody in the room. Something changed, and she came out. I don't want to say effortlessly, but beautifully and perfectly; she went right on my tummy, and I've been ecstatic ever since.

Before she was born, I told my boyfriend, "She's going to either look very familiar or very unfamiliar. Either it's going to be staggering, that 'of course it's you,' or staggering that this person came out of me." When she first came out, she looked so much like this picture that I've grown up looking at. It was the one newborn infant picture my parents had of me. When I looked at her, it was the same face. It was just bizarre. I knew I was going to have to work at not projecting myself all over her. When I saw her I thought, *Oh, God, I'm really going to have to remind myself that she's not me.* She's some person I don't know yet—someone I'm supposed to help her become. It's pretty startling. My dad came into the room about an hour later, and said, "She looks like you." She's now becoming more herself, a combination of her father and me and her grandparents.

One thing I deeply wish for her is to find a way to love every part of herself and to have a real feeling that there's something bigger than her mother or her father that sustains her and supports her. When I went through some difficult times, I recognized that you have to lose the thing you think sustains you in order to realize that something bigger sustains you. If I could give my daughter something, it would be knowing that from as early as possible. But maybe living it is the only way we can really learn it.

Kitty Carlisle Hart

Born Catherine Conn in New Orleans, Louisiana, in 1910, Kitty Carlisle Hart received her early education in Switzerland, followed by study at the Sorbonne, the London School of Economics, and the Royal Academy of Dramatic Art. She graduated to Broadway in 1933, appearing in several operettas and musical comedies staged during the 1930s and '40s. Her films span decades, from Murder at the Vanities *(1934) and* A Night at the Opera *(1935) to Woody Allen's* Radio Days *(1987) and* Six Degrees of Separation *(1993). On television, she was best known for her twenty-three-year stint as a game-show panelist on* To Tell the Truth. *In the opera world, she had the title role in the American premiere of Benjamin Britten's* The Rape of Lucretia *(1948) and made her debut at the Metropolitan Opera in 1967 as Prince Orlofsky in* Die Fledermaus. *In 1983, she returned to the stage in a revival of* On Your Toes. *She was married to playwright Moss Hart from 1946 until his death in 1961. Her autobiography,* Kitty, *was published by Doubleday in 1988.*

ONE DAY, MY MOTHER was in the kitchen for the first time in her whole life, helping me with my lunch box. I don't know why she chose that moment to help, but it was very useful, because the cook went mad, picked up a carving knife, and started after Mother and me. The back stairs were right there in the pantry, and my mother grabbed me by the hand, pulled me down the stairs, and shouted to all the people who were in the house. There were painters, there was my aunt, there was another relative, and there was my mother and me. In those days, we had servants even though we weren't very rich. Everybody gathered in the back of the house, and my mother boosted me up onto the sink to a very high window, and I yelled out the window for the neighbors to call the police. Meanwhile the cook is raging outside, saying, "I know where Dr. Conn's gun is, and I'm going to get it, and I'm going to shoot the lock off this door, and I'm going to kill everybody in the room." Finally the police came, and my mother decided that this was such a traumatic experience that she would do something that she disapproved of and had never done before. She took me to the movies.

I had never been to a movie. I had been to the symphony at night, all dressed up; I'd been to all kinds of concerts, but never to the movies. It was Charlie Chaplin, and we got there, and you know in those days, in 1918 or 1920, it was just a room. So we went to the movies, and everybody was laughing and having a good time, and I couldn't see anything because I'm nearsighted, so I didn't laugh. My mother, being very smart, decided that there was something wrong with my eyes. She took me to the doctor, and I got glasses. For the first time, I saw every little leaf on every tree—it was a revelation. So out of a terrible thing came the best thing that ever happened to me. But my mother wouldn't let me wear my glasses unless it was urgent, because, she said, "People who wear glass get squinty-eyed, and I don't want you to be squinty-eyed." That's the story of my eyes. I still have glasses, but I can read the finest print without them.

At that time, I was Catherine Conn, C-O-N-N. In France and in French, it's a very naughty word. I cannot tell you how dreadful it was in Paris with that name. It had never been changed, so the minute I went onstage, I picked a name from the telephone book. I turned into Kitty Carlisle overnight, and my mother turned into Mrs. Carlisle. I thought that "Kitty Carlisle" was very euphonious.

I never really stood up to my mother, even when I was married and had a child. My mother would call me up—no, my mother never called me up; I called her every day—and she would reduce me to a blithering idiot within five minutes. Moss would imitate me. He would say, "I hear you talking to your mother, and you sound like this: 'Mama, I didn't mean it, I didn't mean it, I'm sorry.'" Can you imagine? One tug on the umbilical cord and I was like a child.

When I was traveling with my mother, I was like Sancho Panza—I had to carry the bags and make sure they got out of the baggage compartment. My mother would stalk out of the trains like an empress in exile. She would stand on the platform waiting for the bags, and I would get them out. I learned to call for a porter in every language. I also hated the fact that when she had one of her fits, she would take to her bed. It didn't matter what was at stake. Sometimes I had to receive fifteen grown-ups for tea and make sure that the tea and the cookies were there. Getting stuff in Paris was not like going to the grocery store here. You had to assemble everything separately. You didn't have an icebox, so it was not easy.

She started locking me out of her hotel room when I was about thirteen. Because I offended her. I always offended her. She said I looked down my nose at her. I spent the whole day on the back stairs with the valets, the maids, and the cooks because I couldn't get into my room. I couldn't go downstairs with the same clothes I had gone to breakfast in, so I sat on the back stairs. I'd take a little flower here and a little flower there, and I would make a little bouquet and put it by the door. I would scratch very gently at the door. When I saw that the flowers had been taken, I would knock and she would let me in. She said I was bad, and I cried, and then she kissed me.

But she did wonderful things too. One day when I was about fourteen, she said, "You know what? I'm going to put a little rouge on your cheeks." She transformed me with just that much; I was a different person. I had gotten to be pretty. I couldn't get over it.

Boys and girls were raised completely differently. Girls were told that we had something to prize—our virginity. We were not allowed to think about anything else. The boys were running wild and doing whatever they wanted to do. When I was about twenty-five, I said to my mother, "When can I have a lover?" And she said, "We'll talk about that next year."

When she was dying, Moss had to go to London because

he was producing *My Fair Lady* with Julie Andrews, and the show was going to open at the Drury Lane Theatre. So he went but my mother was very, very sick. I would go see her every morning, and I would bring my knitting, and I would sit there, and we would talk. We talked in a way we had never talked before. It was even-steven. I was not a little child, I was a grown woman, and she was not the mother that I feared. She was adorable, charming, funny. Oh, she was funny; that was a saving grace. So we had three weeks of the most wonderful time, and I was there when she died.

No matter what she did while I was growing up, she couldn't crush me. And I'll tell you why. There was a tiny little core way deep inside me, like a little stone, and she couldn't squash it. She couldn't crush it. I don't know where it came from. I sailed through life with a great many handicaps, and now look at me. I'm ninety-three years old, happy as a clam. My children like me, and my grandchildren like me.

Kitty Carlisle Hart

Cora Weiss

Cora Weiss is the president of the Hague Appeal for Peace, an international network devoted to the abolition of war and the integration of peace education into all schools. From childhood, she has fought for the rights of women, for civil rights, and for worldwide peace. She was a cofounder, with hundreds of others, of the Women Strike for Peace, which helped bring about the end of atmospheric nuclear testing. In 1969, she became the director of the Committee of Liaison with Families of Prisoners Detained in Vietnam, which oversaw an exchange of mail between POWs being held in North Vietnam and their families in the U.S. In 2005, Ms. Weiss was named one of the one thousand women nominated for the Nobel Peace Prize.

IN 1961, DAGMAR WILSON, the wife of a British consular officer, and herself an artist in Virginia, woke up one morning and decided that women couldn't afford to have atmospheric nuclear testing anymore because it was going to kill our children. The radioactive fallout fell to the grass on the ground, cows ate the grass, the cows were milked, our kids drank the milk, and the strontium-90 got into their teeth. So she called a meeting and said, "We've got to do something to stop this."

I went to the meeting and became one of many early founders of Women Strike for Peace. We were credited by President Kennedy with getting a treaty passed to ban atmospheric nuclear tests. We didn't have the scientific knowledge or the imagination to know that when you banned testing in the atmosphere, it just drove it underground. So that's why I call it the Half-Ban Treaty, because it only banned half the tests.

In 1964–65, Cardinal Spellman took a check to South Korea to hire troops to set up strategic hamlets in South Vietnam, and the Vietnam War was on. That was when it became absolutely clear that the world couldn't afford war anymore, because of the nature of weaponry. There were just too many nuclear weapons, and it was just too dangerous, to say nothing of wrongness, the illegality, the immorality of the war against Vietnam.

Women Strike was brought before the House Un-American Activities Committee. We walked in with flowers to present to all those dreadful men, to throw them off balance, and it succeeded.

After that, we started the Committee of Liaison. We went to Canada to meet with women from Vietnam who were barred from coming into the United States. It was a very dramatic event. The Canadian customs officers tried to stop us. We have great pictures of them putting up their hands to halt us. These days, they would pull out their guns, but somehow we got in.

It was July 4, and we were sitting in a field, licking ice cream cones, on a farm with Vietnamese women. We were all about the same age, all young mothers. These were very courageous women. Many had walked from the South to the North in order to get out. At the end of that weekend, as we licked ice cream cones, they invited me to put together a group of three to go to Vietnam. That was 1969, the height of the bombing, the height of the war. I'd never let my kids do something like that today.

There was no question about my going. I cooked enough food to leave in the freezer for my kids and my husband. Casseroles—those were the years of casseroles, before takeout. I cooked stews and left messages on them saying, "Put in the oven at 350 for an hour."

In December 1969, I left with Ethel Taylor and Madeline Duckles for Vietnam. We carried with us a proposal to the Vietnamese women, who were our hosts, to create a committee to work on the question of prisoners of war. At that time, Nixon had told the world that the reason we were continuing the fight was to free our prisoners of war, who were being tortured in the North. The war now became an issue of prisoners. Together with a group of others, including men, we created the Committee of Liaison with Servicemen Detained in North Vietnam. I was named the executive director.

The idea was to bring mail in from the prisoners of war to establish a list of who was dead and who was alive. Our proposal was to the Vietnamese people, not to the government, not to the military, because it's illegal to negotiate with a foreign government during wartime. We said that we would be willing to bring mail back by hand, because obviously it wasn't working through the regular mail. It was being interrupted deliberately. We came back with 330 letters from POWs being held in Hanoi, the first time there was concrete proof there were that many POWs alive.

We had a press conference which was very amusing, because there were all these guys in basketball jackets sitting in the front. I knew damn well they weren't press. They weren't journalists, because journalists don't wear those kinds of jackets. They were from the CIA and the FBI and the DIA and other military branches. I was known as the housewife from the Bronx; that's what Judge Julius Hoffman called me at the trial of Tom Hayden when I came back from Vietnam. The witness from the Bronx. When I was working on African and civil-rights issues, one paper called me the black housewife from the Bronx. They couldn't believe that a white person would do what I was doing. Anyway, this housewife from the Bronx came back and had a press conference in California and revealed all this information about who was alive in the Hanoi prison camp.

Walter Cronkite carried the news that night but refused to do a photo shot. There was no photo of the press conference. I've often wondered why. But the press that we got all over the United States was incredible. It was very embarrassing to Washington, the fact that we were getting information they couldn't get. And we could demonstrate that what they were saying and doing was lies.

I now head the Hague Appeal for Peace, which calls for the abolition of war and the integration of peace education, the study of alternatives to violence, in all schools. The question is, if we could rid Africa of apartheid, why not war? If we could get rid of slavery, why not war? If we could get rid of colonialism, why not war? And my dream now is to put war on the shelf of history with colonialism, apartheid, and slavery. And I'm no longer considered a crazy woman for saying that.

This whole thing has to do with my three children, born in 1958, 1960, and 1962. I was very young, twenty-four, when I had my first child. One child after the other. It was very clear that the world was too dangerous for them, and I had to do something for their security. And that, of course, became for *everyone's* security, for every child. I wasn't just being selfish. I took my kids with me to Women Strike for Peace meetings, and they learned how to lick stamps, just like I did. They were in on every demonstration. It was part of growing up to participate in all of our activities. Fast-forward to having five grandchildren; I absolutely can't bear the thought of them living with the Bush doctrine of preemption with all the nuclear weapons.

Eleanor Roosevelt talked about it when she said that boys find war exciting, so we have to find another form of excitement for boys. You don't have to be a woman to be for the abolition of war, but you have to have a little feminist consciousness. It would be nice if in my lifetime I could see a few results. We thought we were gaining for a while. It's hard to realize that you have to keep at it. A little success doesn't mean you can stop.

The other reason I don't stop is that I don't know what else to do. When I get up in the morning, this is what I do. I won't hide my feelings that it's uphill. I'll quote Bill Coffin, my friend and mentor, when he wrote in the *Nation*, "Despair is not an option." You have to be pretty optimistic to think that.

Conflict is good. Armed conflict is terrible. Violent conflict is terrible. No matter what else you do, you have to protect your kids. It's not just war. It's armed violence. Everywhere.

Cora Weiss

Lily Tomlin

As a student at Wayne State University, Lily Tomlin performed in theatre-department productions, student-directed projects, and local coffee-houses. After leaving college, she became a regular on the television show Rowan and Martin's Laugh-In, *where she created a number of her enduring characters. She has participated in a multitude of television projects and appeared in many films in a variety of roles, including* Nashville, All of Me, Big Business, *and* The Incredible Shrinking Woman. *In 2003, she won the Mark Twain Prize for American Humor.*

I WAS A FOURTEEN-YEAR-OLD usherette in Detroit when *Gentlemen Prefer Blondes* was playing. An older couple was leaving in the middle of the movie while Jane Russell and Marilyn Monroe were singing and jiggling on the screen. The wife said to the husband, who kept lingering, not wanting to tear his eyes away, "Oh, come on, they don't have any talent anyway." And he said, "They don't need any."

Lily Tomlin

Tawni O'Dell

Tawni O'Dell, a western Pennsylvania native, earned a degree in journalism from Northwestern University. She is the author of Back Roads, *published in 1999, and* Coal Run, *2004.* Back Roads *spent nine weeks on the* New York Times *bestseller list and was an Oprah Book Club pick and a Book-of-the-Month Club Main Selection. She has two children and lives with her husband in Illinois.*

ONE OF MY BEST FRIENDS when I was ten was a kid named Randy. I can't tell you when, where, or how I first met him. We didn't go to school together. He lived near my grandparents, who lived out in the country. My grandfather was a banker in a neighboring small town and seemed to know every living soul within a fifty-mile radius. My grandmother was a homemaker. I spent a lot of time living with them when my teenage parents were trying to get on their feet, both working full-time jobs. By the time I was ten, I had a six-year-old little sister and my dad was a banker too, in a different town. He made a good living, good enough that Mom didn't have to be a secretary anymore and could stay home with my sister and me, but I still spent lots of weekends and a big part of the summer with my grandparents.

I didn't know much about Randy's family or his home life. He wasn't much of a talker. What I was able to gather from my grandparents was that his mother "tried hard" to raise decent children (six of them) and his father was an ex-miner who was on permanent disability even though no one was quite sure what his injury was. The only positive thing I ever heard my grandfather say about Randy's dad was that when Grandpa went out to his house to tell him his truck was about to be repossessed, he didn't take a swing at my grandfather. I gathered from the expression on my grandfather's face as he said this that it was high praise for Randy's dad.

Randy was poor. I knew this because I had only ever seen him wear two different shirts and one pair of jeans, and none of it fit him well, and also by the way he ate when my grandma would sit us down at the kitchen table in the middle of the afternoon and give us a piece of pie. He ate mechanically, with total concentration, the way a dog did. He always praised Grandma's cooking when he was done, but I could tell he found no enjoyment in eating. There was never satisfaction in his eyes. He never smiled. He was grateful but not happy, filled up but not full.

It was important to me that I could do everything that Randy could do. I was a classic tomboy. I grew up in the early 1970s in the coal-mining region of western Pennsylvania, and the advances toward equality of the sexes that were occurring elsewhere in the nation—ending discrimination in the workplace, equal pay for equal jobs, abortion rights, the sexual revolution—weren't occurring here. My hometown in the 1970s was still firmly entrenched in the 1950s (and if you go back there now, it's like being in the 1970s). Most of the girls who were graduating high school when I was a little kid would end up getting married and having babies. The more glamorous, independent ones would aspire to be secretaries or hairdressers. And the ones who did go to college usually were more concerned about dating than classes.

I didn't want any part of being a girl if this was what being a girl meant. Boys could play any sport they wanted. They could be dirty. They could wear ball caps and torn jeans. They could swear. They got to be in charge of everything. And they could be anything they wanted to be when they grew up—from baseball players to secret agents.

Sure, a few positive female role models were beginning to appear in pop culture. Laurie Partridge got off some good zingers at Keith's expense now and then, and when Pinky Tuscadero arrived on the scene in *Happy Days* and even Fonzie's charms couldn't convince her to give up her life on the road as a stunt motorcycle driver, I felt new hope for our gender. But in general the choices seemed very straightforward to me as a child. Boys had all the fun and all the power and all the freedom. Girls could marry Starsky; boys could *be* Starsky.

So I decided to be a boy, and I was pretty good at it. I emulated guys like Randy. I admired his gusto and his guts. He would undertake any challenge, no matter how dangerous or stupid. During our adventures together, there hadn't been anything he was able to do that I hadn't been able to do too. I could climb as high as he could. I stayed on the railroad tracks as long as he did when we heard a train coming. I could ride my bike as fast. I waded into the muck at the bottom of a creek where we both knew there could be leeches. I could almost throw a baseball as far. And I could almost beat him at arm wrestling. I even shot his BB gun. I didn't like shooting the gun, but I was able to do it. That was what was most important to me: that I could do it. I never stopped to think about if I *wanted* to do it. That didn't seem to matter.

One day, we were walking down the road heading for the creek, each of us carrying a Ball jar we were hoping to fill with minnows or crayfish, when we heard this terrible sound. It was a tiny, high-pitched mew so full of pain and terror that it stopped both of us in our tracks, even though the sound was so faint we almost didn't hear it over the crunching of our shoes in the roadside gravel.

We looked behind us in the direction of the sound at the weeds growing on the bank and saw a huge crow tearing at something on the ground. Randy had his BB gun, but he didn't even think to shoot it. He went running toward the crow using it as a club. The bird was so cocky that the sight of a human coming at him didn't bother him at all. Randy had to hit him with the butt of his gun to scare him off. I heard a thud and a squawk before I saw the ugly thing fly away.

I joined Randy, who was looking down into the tall grass and goldenrod. A mangled orange kitten, maybe a couple weeks old, lay panting with his tiny pink tongue hanging out of his mouth, frothy with blood. His blue eyes were open and staring. His little round belly was torn open, and part of his entrails had been tugged out. But he was still alive. Alive enough to cry for help.

"Shit," Randy said.

I turned away. I felt like I was going to puke. Tears welled up in my eyes. The very last thing in the world I wanted to do in front of Randy was cry.

"What are we going to do?" I asked him.

"Ain't nothing we can do," he replied.

"Did that crow do this?"

"Crows don't usually attack something healthy like a hawk will. It might have been sick or hurt, and he saw it and thought it was already roadkill."

That explanation didn't make me like the crow any better.

"Where's its mom?" I asked, and that was it for me. I started to cry.

"Its mom couldn't help," he said simply.

"Can't we help him? We can take him to a vet. My grandma would drive us."

"Nobody can help him. He's gonna die."

"How do you know?"

"He's gonna die," he repeated tonelessly.

I wiped away my tears and looked over at Randy in time to see him turn his gun around so he was holding it the right way again and start to lower the muzzle toward the kitten.

"What are you doing?" I cried out.

"I'm putting him out of his misery."

"You're going to shoot him? You can't do that."

He stared at me over his shoulder. He looked as sad as I felt, but his eyes were dry.

"You'd rather have him lie here and bleed to death? Or

maybe we should walk away, and that crow could come back and finish eating him?" he asked roughly.

"You can't shoot him," I insisted.

He continued looking at me for a moment. Then he turned his head back to the kitten, and with one swift movement he placed the muzzle of the gun somewhere against its soft little body and pulled the trigger.

I can't remember if I said something terrible to him or not. If I called him a name or said I never wanted to see him again. All I know for sure is I ran away crying, back to my grandma's house, and whether I said it or not, I left him thinking I hated him for what he had done.

I was upset with myself for the way I had acted, but I couldn't help it. Not only did I not want that kitten to be shot, I didn't want to change my feeling that way. I was glad I didn't want it to be shot. It felt right. For the first time in my young girl's life, I thought maybe I didn't want to be a boy if being a boy meant I had to be the kind of person who could shoot a kitten.

Sunday evening, before my mom came to pick me up, I was sitting on the back porch helping my grandma shuck corn. My grandfather was standing in their neighbor's driveway talking to the neighbor while he took a break from working on the new garage he was building. My grandfather was not a handy man, but, like all men I knew, he found the tapping of a hammer to be an irresistible lure. It was one of the few things that could make him put down his Sunday paper and get out of his recliner.

I decided to ask Grandma's advice about my dilemma.

"Do you think girls are as good as boys?" I asked her out of the blue.

"What kind of question is that?"

I shrugged in reply.

"When I was a kid, we would've never thought of things like that," she added.

I had heard this kind of response from her before. My mother always rolled her eyes at it. In my mother's opinion, it meant Grandma had been raised in the Dark Ages, when women were told what to do and what to think by men and never questioned the injustice of it then.

"Because you were always taught that boys are better," I volunteered on behalf of my absent mother, and even thought to add in a rather lofty tone, "You think men are superior."

Grandma surprised me by laughing. "I was never taught men are superior. I was taught men are different. And it's a good thing for men and women to be different, and just because we are doesn't make women inferior. All these women nowadays are running around saying they want to be equal to men, but I think a lot of the time they're confusing being equal with men as being the same as men, and those are entirely different things."

"What do you mean?"

"Women nowadays are so concerned about trying to do everything men can do to prove they're as good as men. Well, of course we can do anything men can do. And they can do everything we can do. Except have babies," she added with a smile and a nod. "A woman can be a mechanic. A man can be a baker. Those are skills, and you can have them as a man or a woman. I'm talking about our natures. Our natures are different. And that's the way it should be."

I watched her hands—old before their time from all the years of hard work and the arthritis already beginning to settle into her knuckles—rip away a handful of green leaves and yellow corn silk, then gesture with it toward my grandfather, making a tour of the half-built garage.

"Where would we be if women stopped wanting to take care of things and men stopped wanting to build things?" she asked me.

I didn't visit my grandparents for a couple weeks after that, so I didn't see Randy. I'm not sure if I wanted to see him. But I spent a lot of time thinking about what my grandma had said and thinking about my own gut feelings about what had happened when he shot that kitten. He didn't want to do it, but he knew it needed to be done, so he did it. In my heart of hearts, I knew it needed to be done too, and I also didn't want to do it; the difference was, I couldn't do it. Was it because I was a coward, a wimp? Was it in my nature to be weak? Was it in his nature to be a killer?

I decided that my grandma was right about our different natures and that neither one of us was right or wrong, neither one of us was better or worse. If anything, we complemented each other. It was in his nature to build. In my nature to nurture. In his nature to move forward without looking back. In my nature to care for what was already here. He obeyed a sense of duty. I responded to a sense of loss.

I finally saw him again one Saturday afternoon. I was on my grandparents' front porch and saw him walking down the road toward me. I stayed on the porch steps and he stayed down on the road, but he stopped when he got to the house and I stood up when he stopped.

"Hey," he said.

"Hey," I said back.

"Want to go down to the creek?"

"OK."

And that was the end of our estrangement, but possibly not the end of our disagreement. As we started to walk around back to the kitchen to get some jars, I told him, "I think it was a good thing you shot that kitten. It was the best thing to do."

He looked me straight in the eyes, something he rarely did.

"You really think so?" he asked, and I realized that maybe he had been as troubled by what had happened as I had been, but for different reasons.

It suddenly occurred to me that being a boy might not be all fun and games after all.

"Yeah," I told him, then felt compelled to add, "I couldn't have done it."

"I know," he said. "I wouldn't have wanted you to."

Randy and I were friends for another year. Then along came puberty and junior high. I put away my baseball cap and strapped on my first pair of high heels, and there was no looking back for me. I started spending more time with my friends in town and less time at my grandparents' house. I wouldn't have acknowledged it at the time, but the biggest obstacle to our friendship at that point would have probably become the differences in our home lives, not our sexes.

I'm a grown woman of forty now. I like to think I've made my mark in this world of ours that sometimes still feels very much like a "man's world" to me.

I have a son and a daughter. I'm trying to raise them both with a sense of equality but not of sameness. It isn't always easy. Things may have improved over time in regard to women's quest for equality with men, but the struggle to redefine our roles in society without losing our identities as women still goes on.

For me, whenever I'm faced with a moment when I'm trying to decide if I should follow my female instincts or if I should try to do what is expected of me as defined by one of my gender-neutral roles, such as single parent, breadwinner, homeowner, bestselling author, or whenever I'm faced with a situation where a man frustrates me with what I consider to be his typically male behavior, I think back to Randy and the time we spent together in our youth. I think about how he was able to pull the trigger and I wasn't, and how I'm glad I wasn't able to do it but I'm glad he was.

Tammi O'Dell

Helen Gurley Brown

An author, publisher, and businesswoman, Helen Gurley Brown was editor in chief of Cosmopolitan *magazine for thirty-two years. During the 1960s, she was an outspoken advocate of women's sexual freedom, claiming that women could have it all, "love, sex, and money." Due to her advocacy, the liberated single woman was often referred to generically as the "Cosmo Girl."*

FOR ME, THE REALLY LUSCIOUS memories of childhood are the games—hide-and-seek, punch the icebox, and kick the can. There were winter games and summer games, and I absolutely adored them all. I still have visions of taking over Bloomingdale's one night, without the crowds, bringing in a bunch of my playmates, and playing one of those hide-and-seek games.

I grew up in Little Rock, Arkansas. It had a hundred thousand people then, so it's a city with the advantage of good schools and good stores, but it's still small enough—just the right-size place to grow up. Every autumn, my father took my sister and me to the state fair. It wasn't so much the rides—the roller coaster, the Ferris wheel, and all that—because those we had every summer. The exhibits and the food and being with my father, whom I loved, that was always a happy thing. My mother never went; it was always my father, my sister, and me.

Other happy memories revolved around a place called Alsop Park. Once a week, we would hike there and make Girl Scout sandwiches. Oh, I would kill for a Girl Scout sandwich, which I will never eat again for as long as I live. It was two graham crackers, and half of a slab of Hershey's chocolate, and melted marshmallows! It was so pleasant on those cold, frisky October-November evenings to go hiking and make Girl Scout sandwiches. In early spring, my father took us to gather wild violets. Most of the violets were pale violet, but every so often they would have deep purple petals—those were a great thrill to come across. Summers were spent up in the Ozarks, where most of my relatives still live. There were the fabulous games of hide-and-seek in my grandmother's house, upstairs in the attic, downstairs, out in the barns for the animals, the sheds—it was marvelous.

When I was young, a friend of mine and I produced plays in which we always had the leading roles and did most of the singing and dancing and acting. Maybe people were kinder then, but I can never remember having a bad audience. These childhood forays into performing were terrific. Each week in school, people were invited to perform, and if you learned the words to a new song, from having gone to see a Ginger Rogers and Fred Astaire movie, you could come in and sing it for everybody. I think I knew the words to everything.

My mother was really the quiet one. She didn't, it seems to me, have a great deal of fun with us. I was more apt to have fun with my father. But my mother was a dedicated child helper; she helped me to grow and mature and always encouraged participation in any kind of competition.

A big thrill was going to the World's Fair in Chicago in 1933. I was eleven, and that was the most glamorous thing I'd ever done in my life. My father had died by then, so my mother took me. I rode on an escalator for the first time, which was just heaven, as you can imagine. I rode up and down all day long, till my mother had to restrain me. We rode on double-decker buses and went to the Shedd Aquarium and the Field Museum, where I saw a mummy for the first time in my life. What an absolutely lovely thing for a mother to have done for a little girl.

I was pretty indulged, I'm afraid. My mother married my father in the days when women didn't work, so she was really restrained from having a job of her own, and she poured much too much of her life into my sister and me, making so many things possible for us. She sewed these exquisite clothes—silk dresses with smocking across the yoke, little sleeves, and embroidered collars. We didn't have much money, but my sister and I always had beautiful Easter outfits. Grosgrain hats with ribbons and flowers, little gloves, Mary Janes and the dress and coat to go with it.

When I was ten years old, my father died. That was rough, of course, because we were close and it changed our entire lives. I thought he was perfect, because he played with my sister and me and had a great personality. Later I found out he wasn't so perfect, as nobody is, but he died before I could find out. He was just snatched, killed in an elevator accident at the state capital building. He got on the elevator—apparently it had just left the landing—and he ran and jumped for it, showing off for some lady who was in the elevator—he apparently was quite a man with the ladies. It trapped him, and he was crushed. It was a terrible tragedy. A tremendous fuss was made, because he was well known. At the time, I was not aware of how much that was going to change our lives. Women didn't work in those days, and he left a very modest amount of insurance. He had had a very promising future; from that point on, we weren't in terribly good shape.

Mother tried to keep that from me. But there was always a kind of sadness in our lives after that. She was overwhelmed and decided to move to Los Angeles because my father's brother lived there and she thought he could help look after us. She uprooted and moved because we were running out of money, but she never let me know that. While we were there, my sister got polio. That was a tragic blow. She was in a wheelchair for sixty years. My mother? Imagine having a child felled with a catastrophic illness—a tragedy that would keep her wheelchair-bound for her lifetime. It strengthened me—I *had* to become stronger. While my sister was in the hospital, I started going to a new school in Los Angeles. I was a good student, joined everything, had almost terminal acne, but still managed to be quite popular.

I was class valedictorian, president of the Scholarship Society, president of the Friendship Society, president of a girls' club, straight A's, and my graduation week in high school was the loveliest week of my life, because the president of the student body took me to the senior prom. Too good to be true, because I wasn't particularly pretty, still had acne, and wasn't the belle of the ball, but I think he quite fell in love with me.

After that, the sledding was quite tough. I didn't go to college and had to start working right away. I wrote to my mother every day for as long as she lived. I talked to her for an hour every Sunday afternoon. That childhood didn't just fall on me; it was because of everything my mother did to give me everything she could. Tears come to my eyes when I think about it. I wish there were a way—it's too late now—to repay all that goodness.

Life has turned out agreeably. Maybe it wouldn't have if there weren't those challenges when I was young, that forced me to learn to make the most of whatever I had, however ample or limited the supply. A more ample, rewarding youth might have made for a less rewarding grown-up-hood.

Helen Gurley Brown

Ma Jaya

Ma Jaya Sati Bhagavati is an American-born spiritual teacher. She is widely known for her compassionate work, serving those who are suffering with AIDS, the homeless, the poor, and anyone in need. In 1972, Ma had a spiritual experience that awakened her to her true purpose—"to teach all ways." Her personal journey led her to the teachings of the Hindu saint Sri Nityananda and eventually to her guru, Neem Karoli Baba, whose influence created the foundation for her teaching, which encourages spiritually exploring personal transformation, an embracing love for God, and unconditional love and service to others.

WHEN I WAS A LITTLE GIRL, I was left all alone. It was 1945. I was five or six years old, and I was left in a position of powerlessness. I was running down Brighton Beach Avenue, Coney Island Avenue, to the boardwalk when I bumped into love incarnate. Big Henry was a large black man, way over six foot four, and I bashed right into him under the boards.

"Hey, girl, where you going?" he asked me.

"Leave me the fuck alone," I told him.

"I'm going to put sand in your mouth, I'm going to put

soap in your mouth right now," he said. "Sand or soap—whatever I can get."

Then this other old man came over—I say old, but both men must have been in their late twenties or early thirties—he had crutches, and he said, "Get away from that child. Put that child down."

I got so interested in this conversation.

"Do you want to die? Do you want to be skinned?" Big Henry said. "I ain't putting this child down." And then, turning to me, "Where is your mother?"

With his attention, we just became instant lovers of the moment, and I considered myself one of the luckiest human beings. I knew that there had to be a God to bring these people into my life. To this day, sixty years later, it brings tears to my eyes that the circumstances of karma all came together there.

My mother was dying in Coney Island Hospital, and she said to me—how she knew, I don't know, to this day I don't know—but she said, "You're reaching a certain age now that you can't be with your black folks." I just looked at her in shock. I couldn't believe it. But I never felt powerless for too long. It was only from those very first moments of my life in 1945 till the moment I bumped into that giant and his crew—Chickie and Chews—who were both prostitutes, drug addicts, and alcoholics. Those four gathered around me under the penalty of death, even though we were in the North, because they had a little white girl sleeping in a box with a black man. That taught me so many things: the sharing, no throwaway people, what I have is yours. Do something and make people smile.

Every single day was an adventure with them. As the day would begin, we'd go out very early in the morning, 'cause once the sun came up in the summer, they usually didn't leave the covering of the boardwalks. So before the cleaning trucks came to clean, we'd go collect bottles. Then we'd bring them back, and I would split the deposit money with them. They'd get booze and I'd have a few pennies for myself. We lived off the bottles in the summer. We'd sit in the night beneath the stars under the boardwalk and have the best picnic you could imagine. We'd just cut up. They were always drunk, even though I didn't know what that was, to be drunk. I would just say, "They're in that way again." It was heaven on earth to me. If you just wore a bathing suit, nobody knew if you were poor or if you were rich. In the winter, the joggers on the board-walk would always drop money through the cracks, so we had a few pennies that we all shared.

They used to call me Girl Child: "Hey, Girl Child." They gave me my accent, is between a black person and a Jew and a Brooklynite. It was a community, but it wasn't all roses, it wasn't all peaches—the things that I saw at times didn't make sense to me. There were some horrible things under-neath there. But Big Henry said to me, "You've got to listen to people's stories." He banged that into me every single day.

In those four short years, I learned everything I really needed to know and how I have to be.

Ma Jaya Sati Bhagavati

Maria Shriver

Born November 6, 1955, in Chicago, Maria Shriver is the only daughter of Eunice Kennedy and Sargent Shriver. The niece of John F. Kennedy and Robert Kennedy, she is the wife of current California governor Arnold Schwarzenegger. After graduating from Georgetown University, she worked for twenty-five years as a television journalist, winning both Peabody and Emmy Awards. She is the author of Ten Things I Wish I'd Known—Before I Went into the Real World, And One More Thing Before You Go . . . , *as well as the children's books* What's Wrong with Timmy?, What's Heaven?, *and* what's Happening to Grandpa? *She and her husband have two daughters and two sons.*

MY STORY IS ABOUT growing up equal. My mother, the woman I most admire, pushed me to do everything my four brothers did. If they went to the baseball game with my dad, I went to the baseball game with my dad. If they took tennis lessons, I took tennis lessons. If they played football, I played football. I tried to do all the sports that were offered, but I did have one area that was my own—I was a competitive rider, with a little buckskin pony named Miss Buck, whom I rode every day and showed almost every weekend. My brothers didn't mess with me, because I was better at it than they were. Riding gave me a place to go that was away from them, an outlet, and that was critical for me.

My story is also about learning to march to your own drummer. My mother marched to her own drummer. She was an original. None of my friends had a mother like mine, something I was very conscious of from an early age. She drove a station wagon or a Jeep or an open Lincoln that had dogs and boys in it. As founder of the Special Olympics, she had people with mental disabilities in the house all the time, and after dinner she was always in meetings with guys.

Other mothers had their hair done and wore little skirts and carried purses; my mother wore tweed pants, had pencils in her hair, and smoked a cigar. She was a character. I remember feeling conflicted about it, sometimes embarrassed about it, sometimes thinking, *She's cool, but what is she? I don't really see any other women like her.* She always said to me, "You may be beautiful, but it's going to go. Concentrate on your brains." Now, as I become older, I realize how cool and unique she was, but I definitely thought there was something off about it, growing up. You know something is different when the other girls are shopping and having their nails done. Meanwhile your one uncle is president, another is the attorney general, your father runs the Peace Corps, and your mother has people with mental disabilities in your backyard. I thought my whole upbringing was a little bit different, so I assumed that my mother was just part of the overall package.

As an adult, I'm learning to do those female things. I always used to look down on it and view it as soft, because I didn't have that experience in my own house. Now that I'm raising two daughters, I try to give them a sense of equality and opportunity yet also let them know that it's okay to want to look and be feminine—but you also have to be strong. It's a challenging message to give to girls, because you don't want them to be just one way or the other. You have to make both things available and allow them to be who they are, as opposed to who you want them to be. It's tough, because there are so many mixed messages for girls. I'm saying, "Be strong, do your own thing."

Family was a critical component in my growing up. It was very clannish, very familial. Everything was about family, about giving back and how you were going to change the world. Being stalwart East Coast Irish, you didn't come home looking for sympathy; there wasn't a lot of that in my house. My parents didn't do it, my brothers sure didn't do it. You made your own way. The attitude was, *Be tough.* Don't sit around and bemoan your situation. Don't even really try to make sense of it. It's not about fair; fair isn't in the equation. Just pick up your head, square your shoulders, move forward, and do something that helps people.

When I was fifteen, my parents sent me to Tunisia for the summer to live and work with Peace Corps volunteers and then again, at sixteen, to Senegal. They didn't think it through the way a parent does today. They just said, "This is going to be a good experience. You'll live with an Arab family in Tunis. Call us when it's finished." They felt I could handle it, and if I couldn't, I'd better figure out how to.

I've tried to address the strong message that ran throughout my childhood—"What are you doing to help?"—through my books and my journalism. My choice of journalism was defined my own way and was in many ways a good fit for me. It was creative, and I've always felt creative in my writing and in my mind, thinking in stories. And it's competitive, immediate, and certainly very male-oriented. Almost everybody in the newsroom was a man when I started. Having been raised to feel accepted as an equal, I wasn't flustered by that at all. I was used to a houseful of guys. Used to their competitiveness, their testosterone, and their humor. None of it threw me off. I grew up thinking I deserved to be in the room, any room. My father used to say to me, "Those people who are in the room are damn lucky you're in there with them."

When you go into journalism, the questions are, Do you want to be a White House correspondent? Do you want to be this? Do you want to be that? But I never felt easily pegged. I never wanted to be any one thing. Even now, as first lady, I'm asked, Can you pick one cause? I can't. I'm not a one-note person. I don't think that way. I always look at a very big canvas.

After all, consider the example my mother set: You can march to your own drummer. You can be an original. You don't have to fall in line. You don't have to wear those suits or drive that car, get your hair done or be that kind of a wife. Make it up, be your own creation, be your own original.

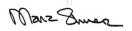

Meryl Streep

Born in 1949 in Summit, New Jersey, Meryl Streep appeared off-Broadway while still attending Vassar College. Graduating in 1971, she joined the Green Mountain Summer Repertory Group (Woodstock, Vermont), where she acted and directed. After essaying a wide variety of memorable characters at the Yale Repertory Company, she arrived in New York to deliver award-winning theater performances and then made her film debut in Julia *(1977). Beginning with* The Deer Hunter *(1978), she has been nominated for Academy Awards thirteen times, winning for* Kramer vs. Kramer *(1979) and* Sophie's Choice *(1982). She is a five-time Golden Globe winner, including one for her performance as Ethel Rosenberg and other characters in the* Angels in America *(2003) miniseries.*

I FELT SAFE AS A CHILD. The question of feeling precarious in any way never arose until I was about eleven. I was in a post office with my mother, and I saw a picture of a child who had been stolen, a boy about seven years old. That was a very unusual thing in those days. There weren't people on milk cartons and missing-children hotlines, and I remember being really interested and asking my mother, "Well, how did that child get taken?" It was very weird. Under the picture, it said, "Have you seen anything relating to this child?" Nobody knew anything about the boy. How could somebody not know to whom this child belonged? The idea that that could happen was really horrible. I asked my mom about the picture, and she explained to me that there were people who kidnapped children. She told me about the Lindbergh baby, and then I understood that there were some bad guys out there. It's a thing that never occurred to me until that moment.

I was the oldest in my family, with two little brothers. My littler brother was four years younger than I was, and I took care of him. When he was very young, he was teased because he had big ears. He eventually grew into them, but back then the kids made fun of him. That was the first time I got really mad at somebody, and I beat up the kids who were making fun of him. I got into trouble for it, but I loved him so much. He was my baby, and I just couldn't bear that they were calling him names. He was kind of spoiled by everybody because he was the last. That happens in my family now.

As kids, we had pets, though ours were sort of disastrous. We had a sweet dog that ran away or was picked up. He was a purebred and just disappeared one day. We got a couple of replacements, but both of them were mildly vicious. One ate all the neighbor's ducks—it was awful and very bloody and gruesome. That dog found another home on a dairy farm somewhere far out in the wilds of New Jersey.

My mother was very visual; she was a commercial artist. We all drew, and she taught me to sew and knit. I found a picture of me the other day in my eighth-grade Easter suit, which I made myself. It was navy blue and had white piping on the cuffs and the collar. It was really good-looking. I remember making it and feeling very accomplished.

As a girl, I remember really liking the feeling of being pretty. It was sort of thrilling and could put a spring in your step. Of course, it was always accompanied by that tiny little demon voice that said, "No, you're not pretty." But there were certain mornings you would go out—the sun was shining, your hair was clean, you had a new pair of shoes, and you just felt great.

There was a girl who lived up the street who had this Native American sampler, a cross-stitch on her wall, and it said, "Do not judge another man until you have walked a mile in his moccasins." That was something that really stuck with me—to walk in somebody else's shoes, to feel like somebody else. Are we the same? Or are we different?

There was a big moment that was very important. My fifth-grade teacher asked me to read the class a story that I had written. They didn't normally ask people to read things, so I thought it was fairly unusual that I had to read it. I got up thinking, *Is this a punishment?* But I liked my story because it was funny, so I read it, and everybody was roaring with laughter. I got a real zip from that. It was a science-fiction story that had humor and a lot of alliteration and silly things in it. I'm sure it was heavily influenced by Dr. Seuss. There's nothing like getting laughs to make you think differently about yourself.

From an early age, I started doing imitations of people.

I'm sure some of them were cruel. We learn kindness as we go along. It was always to get a laugh from my brothers or my parents or my friends. The one time I was truly aware of observing somebody was with my grandmother. I looked really hard at her hands and her feet and her neck to see if that was the way I was going to be. I went home and got my mother's eyebrow pencil, and I drew all the lines that I had memorized from my grandmother's face on my own face and took a picture of it. It looks like me in *Angels in America* now. It looks like Hannah Pitt.

I loved my grandmother very much; she was a very funny, elegant lady who was full of stories. One of the strongest memories I have is when I was fifteen, sitting on the floor cross-legged, and she looked at me—she was eighty-six—and she said, "You know, in my mind I can do that. I can sit right on the floor. If I close my eyes, I can get right down next to you and cross my legs, really I can. In my mind I still can. I can still turn a somersault, because I feel in my mind like I'm fifteen." She was saying to me, "I look like this, but I'm like you." So in *my* mind I thought, *I look like me, but I feel like her.* And since my mother died, I've felt so many times when I'm walking that she's completely in my body. I don't know how to describe it, but I feel that not only do I recognize her walk in my walk but sometimes I feel like *I'm her walking.* It's just very visceral. Can we feel our DNA? I don't know.

When I was in high school, I felt completely insecure. But at the same time, I was fairly bossy, which is a nice combination. In terms of my femaleness, in high school I learned how to impersonate a woman, a girl, a teenager. How to look, how to walk, and how to behave with boys. Boys were the context in which the whole female world arranged itself. We didn't have any sports programs for girls at our school. There was football for the boys, and girls could be cheerleaders. That was the most athletic you could be, and that's what I did. How you dressed and how you put your hair together were fairly rigorously defined. Everybody tried to look like people on the cover of *Seventeen*. You were destined to be unhappy if you looked at those magazines, which is still true.

In high school, I realized there was a strategy one could employ to be more palatable in mixed company, both to girls and boys. That had to do with curbing your natural tendency to drive the conversation or to be too emphatic in expressing your points. I guess it's a way of learning gracefulness. Or maybe it was phoniness. I think they're equal components, parts of learning how to be sociable. On the other hand, I recognized that there was a distinctively feminine component that had to do with deferring, which I really didn't like. I could see why I had to do it and how effective it was. It had to do with laughing at everything a boy would say, and agreeing more than being contentious. Deflecting more difficult topics and being girly. I certainly got more dates when I acted this way, no question about it.

I really only felt like myself when I got to college. I went to Vassar, an all-women's college at that time, and I think the fact that there were no men had something to do with how I felt in my own skin and in myself. Because there wasn't a mold or thing you were supposed to be fitting into. You were supposed to find your own individuality and be yourself. High school was all about conforming to existing ideals, and college was all about making up your own ideal and who you wanted to be.

I didn't look at *Seventeen* or any of those magazines once I went to college. I didn't think about that stuff. I remember once I didn't wash my hair for three weeks. It was quite a radical thing to do. I turned away from all that—the tyranny of how you look—which was what ruled in high school, and then after college it ruled again. It turns out that the great big world is like high school. But there was a little halcyon moment that was Vassar, where those things didn't matter and we concentrated on other stuff.

You had to fight for your space there. I really liked that, You had to think about what you really believed, instead of figuring out what was *nice* to believe. I remember thinking it was such a relief to be myself, to laugh too loud or be coarse. The language we used was appalling, but it was just a heady kind of delirious freedom, real freedom.

It was a door into liberation, liberation of the personality. It's always better to be authentically yourself. All these things are a part of learning how to live with other people.

Acknowledgments

My heartfelt thanks—

To the contributors, who gave of their time and hearts, for their generosity.

To Bill Adler Books: Bill and Gloria Adler, Jan Crozier, and Allen Appel; to Adler & Robin Books: Bill Adler Jr., Peggy Robin, and Jeanne Welsh.

To brilliant editor Mary Ellen O'Neill, fierce midwife of this book; Will Schwalbe for steering the ship; Brenda Copeland for being a superb adoptive editor; Miriam Wenger for her deep commitment to the project; and Dana Beck for artful writing, shaping, organizing, and co-creating,

To those who helped me focus: Jennifer Manocherian, for her infernal honesty, creativity, and brilliant editing; Tamara Weiss; Minna Proctor; and Dean Ericson, my partner in everything.

To my family's females, the ever-changing swirl of becoming: sisters Emily, Amanda, Beth, and Naomi; aunts Leonore and Shirley; cousins Naomi, Eliza, Mia, Danica, Thea, Miranda, Zoey, Beatrice, Lily, Eve, Tubby, Sarah, Lynn Miriam, Barbara, and Anjali; nieces Katin and Rowan. Each of you inspires me.

To Martha Buchanan, my mentor in becoming and evolving with grace; to Sioux Eagle, Anne Glauber, and Deb Newman for understanding and loving me; to Cristina Torre for being my a.f.

To the women of Rwanda, especially Kaliza Karuretwa, Aurea Kayiganway, Pascasie Mukamulingo, Francoise Mukagihana, Joy Ndungutse, Janet Nkubana, for being examples of courage, determination, and grace.

To my miraculous father for giving me the inspiration, chutzpah, and freedom to become myself.

Beneficiary Organizations

Equality Now works for the protection and promotion of the human rights of women around the world. In collaboration with national women's rights organizations and individual activists, Equality Now documents violence and discrimination against women and adds an international action overlay to support their efforts to advance equality rights and defend individual women who are suffering abuse. Issues of urgent concern to Equality Now include rape, domestic violence, reproductive rights, trafficking of women, female genital mutilation, and the denial of equal access to economic opportunity and political participation. *www.equalitynow.org*

The Family Violence Prevention Fund (FVPF) has, for more than two decades, pioneered new strategies and developed model programs to stop violence against women and children. Recognized internationally as one of the foremost leaders in violence prevention, the FVPF has helped advance the rights of women and children everywhere through public policy, awareness and action campaigns, leadership development especially among women of color and immigrant women, and specialized training programs for professionals such as judges, doctors, employers, police, prosecutors, teachers, and even coaches. The

FVPF is committed to building a society where all of our daughters, sisters, mothers, aunts, and friends are safe, healthy, respected, and empowered to pursue whatever it is that they wish to achieve in life without the fear or threat of violence, so that they may succeed and truly become themselves. *www.endabuse.org* Tel: 415-252-8900

INTERSECT-Worldwide employs a new organizing principle for social mobilizations through powerful, multi-disciplinary Intersect Coalitions across Africa and India where HIV and violence against women and girls run rampant. These Coalitions engage in innovative approaches to education, law, and public policy and marshal a formidable, visible force to create significant change in the social environment in which these co-epidemics thrive so that social justice, gender parity, and a life of quality and safety replace the current specters of violence and HIV. *www.intersect-worldwide.org*

V-Day is a global movement to end violence against women and girls, founded by Eve Ensler. In 2005, more than 2,500 V-Day benefits of *The Vagina Monologues* took place in the United States and around the world from Ethiopia to China, Indiana to India, Croatia to Finland. V-Day has raised more than $30 million and educated millions about the issue of violence against women and the efforts to end it; crafted international educational, media, and PSA campaigns; reopened shelters; and funded more than 5,000 community-based antiviolence programs and safe houses in Kenya, South Dakota, Egypt, and Iraq. The "V" in V-Day stands for Victory, Valentine, and Vagina. *www.vday.org*